CAPE PLAYS

THE OLD ONES

by the same author

THE WESKER TRILOGY
(Chicken Soup with Barley, Roots,
I'm Talking about Jerusalem)

THE KITCHEN

CHIPS WITH EVERYTHING

THE FOUR SEASONS

THEIR VERY OWN AND GOLDEN CITY

THE FRIENDS

FEARS OF FRAGMENTATION

SIX SUNDAYS IN JANUARY

ARNOLD WESKER

The Old Ones

JONATHAN CAPE
THIRTY BEDFORD SQUARE LONDON

FIRST PUBLISHED 1973

© 1972 BY ARNOLD WESKER

JONATHAN CAPE LTD
30 BEDFORD SQUARE, LONDON WCI

HARDBACK EDITION ISBN O 224 00820 X
PAPERBACK EDITION ISBN O 224 00858 7

PRINTED IN GREAT BRITAIN
BY EBENEZER BAYLIS & SON LTD
THE TRINITY PRESS, WORCESTER, AND LONDON
BOUND BY G. & J. KITCAT LTD, LONDON

This play was first performed at the Royal Court Theatre, London, on August 8th, 1972, under the direction of John Dexter, designed by Douglas Heap, with the following cast:

Emanuel	MAX WALL
Gerda, *Emanuel's wife*	AMELIA BAYNTUN
Boomy, *Emanuel's brother*	GEORGE PRAVDA
Sarah, *Emanuel's sister*	PATIENCE COLLIER
Teressa, *Sarah's friend*	WANDA ROTHA
Millie, *Sarah's friend*	ROSE HILL
Jack, *Sarah's neighbour*	GEORGE TOVEY
Rosa, *Sarah's daughter*	SUSAN ENGEL
Rudi, *Sarah's nephew*	LEONARD FENTON
Martin, *Boomy's son*	JAMES HAZELDINE
Three youths	TERRY BURNS
	STEPHEN GRIVES
	MARTIN SKINNER

For our children
Lindsay Joe, Tanya Jo and Daniel

ERRATA

Page 13, fourth line from bottom should read:
   "whispering to myself"

Page 38, first line should read:
   "One can imagine the whole farm clapped hands, cheering"

Page 53, fifth line from bottom should read:
   "so often held in her gaze—"

CHARACTERS

EMANUEL   aged about 70
GERDA   his wife, about 68
BOOMY   his younger brother
SARAH   his sister, about 71
TERESSA   Sarah's friend, about 68
MILLIE   Sarah's friend, about 71
JACK   Sarah's neighbour, about 72
ROSA   Sarah's daughter, about 32
RUDI   Sarah's nephew (son of a dead sister), about 40
MARTIN   Boomy's son, about 28
3 YOUTHS aged about 16

Everyone except JACK and the THREE YOUTHS happens to
be Jewish; nevertheless this play is essentially about defiant
old age.

THE SETTINGS

There are seven different settings:

The garden and porch of Emanuel's house
Boomy's room in Emanuel's house
Sarah's council flat—the front room
Millie's council flat—the kitchen
Teressa's kitchen/dining room in an old Victorian house
A street
The classroom

I visualise two revolves, one containing three, the other two,
interior sets, with the space between left for a street and the
classroom.

ACT ONE

Scene One

Darkness. Then, the thin light of a hazy, summer dawn, just enough to catch the figure of an old man rushing from a hammock on a porch into a garden.
Which way must he turn, what must he say? He can decide neither.
He screams, a harrowing, confused sound, the pain incomprehensible to him.
Exhausted, he crumbles; the light is growing, the night over.
An old woman limps into sight.

EMANUEL. Warnings! All I can do is cry out warnings. What's that for a life?

GERDA. Torturing yourself again?

EMANUEL. But there's no light.

GERDA. You torturing yourself again?

EMANUEL. Crying out in the darkness. Typical!

GERDA. And you're torturing me also.

EMANUEL. No light, and no one there. Nothing!

    (GERDA *stands by him to cradle his head.*)

GERDA. You think I'm not tired?

EMANUEL. There should be an echo, a coming back of something.

GERDA. It's not enough already?

    (EMANUEL *screams.*)

    MANNY!

    (*He disentangles himself and lumbers about. Frantically he searches the garden. Two stones; he knocks them together, waits between each sad, stinging sound; three times. Searches again. An old kettle, a piece of wood; he rattles the one in the other, rapidly.*

9

Again he crumbles to his knees. Again she comes to him, rocks him in her arms. He moans, full of helpless pity for what seems lost, wasted, irretrievable.)

EMANUEL. Ah! Gerda. I'm reduced to such simple sounds. Noises, that's all.

GERDA. Come, Manny. It's not a way to grow old. Like this? A madman? You're not a madman and you know you're not a madman. Come.

(*He allows himself to be drawn back to the hammock on the porch. She enters the house. He returns to sleep.*
Slowly, the bright sunlight of morning.

GERDA *comes from the house, across the porch, with a tray of tea, toast and boiled eggs. She wears an orthopaedic shoe. A few hours have passed.*)

(*Pouring*) China tea! A new madness. Every morning a thin cup of smelly tea.

EMANUEL. Mornings my mouth is like I've been through a sandstorm. I need a delicate taste.

GERDA. Delicate taste! My delicate man!

(*She slices his eggs.*)

EMANUEL. You know, I must stop sleeping out at nights.

GERDA. Now he's decided.

EMANUEL. It's too cold and I'm too old to camp out.

GERDA. Who says you're too old?

EMANUEL. You're cantankerous, you know that?

GERDA. Cantankerous! Cantankerous! Here, I heard a new quotation on the radio. (*Gives him torn-off piece of paper.*)

EMANUEL. Show me. (*Reading from it*) 'All things fall and are built again. And those that build them again are gay.' Ha, ha! He won't have one to match this, not so early in the morning.

(*He crosses porch to the room and bangs on a wall.*)

You listening? (*Pause.*) You there? Boomy, you awake yet?

BOOMY'S VOICE. I'm awake.

EMANUEL. 'All things fall and are built again. And those that build them again are gay.'

BOOMY'S VOICE. Who wrote it?

EMANUEL (*to* GERDA). Who wrote it?

GERDA. Bates.

EMANUEL. Bates!

BOOMY'S VOICE. Bates?

EMANUEL (*to* GERDA). Bates?

GERDA (*uncertain now*). Gates?

EMANUEL. Gates? (*Pause.*) Yeats, perhaps?

GERDA. Yeats!

EMANUEL (*calling to* BOOMY). Yeats!

   (*Silence.* EMANUEL *interprets silence as victory and is about to return to his breakfast.*)

BOOMY'S VOICE (*mumbling*). ' ... and those that build them again are gay'. (*Pause.*) 'For, alas, what is Contract? If all men were such that a mere spoken or sworn Contract would bind them, all men were then true men, and Government a superfluity. Not what thou and I have promised to each other, but what the balance of our forces can make us perform to each other; that, in so sinful a world as ours, is the thing to be counted on.'

EMANUEL. Who wrote it?

BOOMY'S VOICE. Carlyle.

EMANUEL. Carlyle! Still Carlyle. You've been reading him for two months now. I'll give you three more quotations from him and then you've got to find your proofs of doom from somewhere else. You hear me?

   (*Returns to his breakfast but on the way picks up a tailor's dummy with an uncut suit on it. On the porch he pins and unpins it while eating his breakfast.*)

GERDA (*calling*). Boomy! You want breakfast?

BOOMY'S VOICE. In my room.

GERDA. Come out and eat, it's sunshine outside.

BOOMY'S VOICE. Too hot!

EMANUEL. Get some sun on you.

BOOMY'S VOICE. In my room, please.

EMANUEL. He keeps me alive, my brother. With his philosophy of doom he keeps me alive.

(GERDA *enters the house.*

Alone, shyly, EMANUEL *takes a portable tape-recorder, rewinds it a little and plays back the last snatches of himself singing a Socialist song. Delighted, he turns to a new part and records another, this time Hasidic, song in Yiddish.* He sings into the microphone with gestures as though before an audience — it's obvious this is what he's wanted to do all his life. When finished he winds everything back and replays. He returns to the work on his dummy and talks while listening to himself sing.*)

(*To unseen* GERDA) Your son wants a suit? He shall have a suit. Your grandchildren want coats? They shall have coats. (*Stands back from dummy.*) You know, I once worked with a machiner, Joe! Joe — er — Joe — er — names! I can't remember names. What's the matter with me? Was a time I remembered everything, everything! Anyway. Joe. A rotten machiner. Didn't like the work. You can't do well what you don't like and he was proof. But a talker? An intellect? Mustard! From him I got the habit of reading and through him shaped what I'd read. Between us we should have done great things. Only we didn't. (*Pause.*) Anyway, one day, he looked at my dummy and he said, 'Manny,' he said, 'the other day the dummy spoke to me.' 'Get on with your work,' I tell him, 'we're behind.' 'It spoke,' he said again, 'and it asked me "What of your life?" Imagine! the dummy asked me to justify myself.' 'And did you?' I asked Joe. 'It's very disturbing,' he says, 'not a nice question to be asked.' And that was all. For the

---

* Both these songs, 'Zog Nit Kein Mol' and 'Auf ein veig steit a boym', are recorded by Nehama Lifschitz on CBS S.63626. The first is on side one, no. 5; the second, on side two, no. 1.

rest of the day he said nothing more, absolutely nothing more. (*Pause.*) A man of sweetness and a big forehead. (*Shouting to his brother.*) Boomy! You should work in your old age. Stop thinking so much.

Scene Two

SARAH's *council flat. It is full of healthy pot plants.*
We see the front room and a balcony on which her nephew,
MARTIN, *is erecting the 'Succah'. The 'Succah' is a symbolic*
'tent' with a partly covered roof of branches. We will learn more
about it as the play progresses.
MARTIN *has nailed together a rather shaky wooden frame around*
which he is now pinning a white sheet. SARAH *is passing him the*
pins.
ROSA, *her daughter, is reading aloud from a little book about the*
Jewish festival of 'Succoth'.*

ROSA. 'The festival of Succoth, known as "The Festival of Tabernacles", begins on the 15th day of Tishri, lasts for eight days and is called "The Season of our Joy".'

SARAH. That's how I remember it. Joyful! Your grandfather was a very joyful man. Your Uncle Manny takes after him.

ROSA. 'Judaism recognises the natural instinct of joy and makes no attempt to repress it, but rather to encourage natural self-expression.'

MARTIN. Good! I like that.

ROSA. And I like this. Listen: 'To draw away from a natural instinct of gladness with the fear that gladness might lead to vice is an admission of inability to exercise that restraint which requires strength of character.'

* Isaac Fabricant, *A Guide to Succoth* (London, Vallentine, Mitchell, 1957).

MARTIN. Very Jesuitical.

SARAH (*shaking frame*). It's got a bit of a wobble.

MARTIN. I'm not trained as a 'Succah' maker, Aunt Sarah.

SARAH. But it'll do.

ROSA. 'The Bible, through the law of the Succah, brings man face to face with the realisation of the frailty of human life and the transience of human existence.'

MARTIN. I thought it was a harvest festival.

ROSA. It is. But, says the book, 'In the season of plenty the Jew rejoices in his prosperity and in the rewards which his labours have brought him and is inclined to delude himself into thinking that life is secure and durable.' So the Psalmist warns people who are misled by this fantasy and who, quote, 'trust their wealth and boast themselves in the multitude of their riches', unquote.

MARTIN. Very wise.

ROSA (*to* MARTIN). 'It is essential that the "Succah" is built in a manner which enables it to provide more shade than light; but, because man—' Ah! Mother, you wanted to build the 'Succah'? Then listen to this: 'But because man should not have confidence in his own strength nor in his own fortunes but should place his faith in Divine providence, therefore the covering of the "Succah" with plants and leaves should not be laid on too thickly so that the heaven and the stars should be visible, for, as Psalm XIX says, the heavens declare the "glory of God".'

MARTIN. 'The glory of God'! What do you say to that, Aunty?

SARAH. Let the heavens declare the glory of God, we'll build the 'Succah' to declare the glory of man.

MARTIN. Bravo!

SARAH. And to remember my father.

MARTIN. That's my Sarah.

SARAH. And for your Aunty Gerda who likes these things.

ROSA. But, Mother, that's hypocrisy.

SARAH. She's insulting me again. What's hypocrisy about it?

ROSA. You don't believe.

SARAH. I don't believe.

ROSA. But suddenly! Out of the blue! The rituals of belief.

SARAH. Suddenly! The blue! The rituals of belief.

ROSA. It's not logical.

SARAH. It's not logical.

(*Stubborn pause.*)

ROSA. Actually, maybe it is logical. After all, I suppose it's very human to want to remember your father.

MARTIN. And Aunty Gerda.

SARAH. She's a good girl, my daughter. If you let her argue long enough on her own, she gets to agree with you. (*Picking up an old refrain*) She's got a job as a careers-advisory officer, you know, with the Ministry of Education. Such a profession.

(ROSA *tries to out-talk her by picking out something else to read from the little book.*)

ROSA (*together*) SARAH

'We cannot measure life quantitatively. It is not the number of years but rather the quality that determines whether life is transient or permanent. The Rabbis had this thought in mind when they said: "In one brief hour a man can achieve eternity." '

She went to university, got degrees, honours, I-don't-know-what, but she couldn't decide on a profession for herself so she took up advising others. I'M GOING SHOPPING!

(SARAH *has the last word as she leaves.*

ROSA *joins* MARTIN *to help with the 'Succah'.*)

ROSA. How's Uncle Boomy?

MARTIN. My father and I quarrel. He wants me to stick to my research.

ROSA. And stay out of student politics.

MARTIN. And stay out of student politics. 'You'll make me into a neurotic,' I tell him. 'So what?' he says, 'there's plenty analysts, aren't there?'

ROSA. And you've left Moira and the baby for good?

MARTIN. Who knows what's for good?

ROSA. We've both made a mess of our marriages.

MARTIN. You should've married me.

ROSA. Cousins?

MARTIN. We'd have kept our qualities in the family.

ROSA. And weakened the strain.

MARTIN. Everything has a price.

(*Pause.*)

ROSA (*leafing through the little book*). Do you think *we'll* turn to rituals after fifty?

MARTIN. Ecclesiastes! He keeps quoting Ecclesiastes at me. (*Imitating* Boomy) 'It is better to hear the rebuke of the wise than for a man to hear the song of fools.'*

ROSA (*reading from the little book*). 'Men learned in the law came to the Besht — the founder of Hasidism — on an errand of dispute. "In times gone by," they protested, "there were pious men in great numbers fasting from Sabbath to Sabbath, and inflicting their own bodies with self-devised torments. And now your disciples proclaim it, to all who care to listen, that much fasting is unlawful and self-torment a crime." The Besht answered, "It is the aim and essence of my pilgrimage on earth to show my brethren by living demonstration how one may serve God with merriment and rejoicing. For he who is full of joy is full of love for men and all fellow-creatures." '

* For this and all other quotations from Ecclesiastes, see page 79.

Scene Three

TERESSA's *dishevelled kitchen/dining room. A scrubbed table is
full of books, papers and a typewriter.*
TERESSA, *a heavily built, once beautiful, elderly woman, enters in
her petticoat. A dress is over her arm, a roll of toilet paper in her
hand. She lays the dress over a chair; hoists her petticoat and
proceeds to wrap the toilet roll round her middle.*

TERESSA. You never know when you may need what.
> (*She puts on her dress, moves to a mirror to adjust her hair
> and heavily cosmeticise her face. Then she sits down to think
> what next to do.*
> *Her accent is deeply Slavonic.*)

All dressed up and nowhere to go. (*Pause.*) It's not funny,
darling. If I wasn't an educated woman I'd understand,
but I'm educated! A reader of books! A translator!
> (*She idly reaches for a piece of paper and reads from it.*)

'Wanda Wilczynski was born in 1857 in the market
town of Lashkowitz in Poland. To this town my father
went in terror of his life to sell his goods, and he brought
back news of this strange poetess whom everyone thought
was mad. My father's passion became mine and for this
reason I have felt it a duty to undertake the translation of
her poetry into this the most harmonious of languages.'
'Harmonious'? That's a way to describe the English
language? 'Lyrical'! A better word.
> (*She scribbles the alteration but it's a casual stab at work.*)

Ach! Books! Thoughts! If they live in your head and you
can't use them — useless! Mocking! Fifteen years I've been
translating you, Wanda my darling. (*Moves again to mirror.*)
Look at my face. When did you last see a face that said
so much. It's all there, Teressa, full of lines. And I can tell
you which line is which. (*Pointing*) Disappointment,

bitterness, self-hatred, surprise, fear. Sour—all sour, my darling.

(*She turns away unhappily; then, defiantly*) I want to look beautiful!

(*Shrugs. Moves to cut a slice of bread; eats it with a lump of cheese, indifferently.*)

(*Full mouth*) Silly woman! Silly, silly woman, Teressa. (*Pause.*) What's silly about wanting to be beautiful again? Vanity? It's vain to want to look in a mirror and get pleasure? I tell you, with that kind of pleasure I'd be so generous, so generous and calm and dignified. Sweetness, darling, there's such a sweetness in beauty. Oh dear. Oh dear, dear me. (*Pushes away food.*) Who can eat?

(*She picks up papers again.*)

'Her life was a tragedy. At the age of thirteen she was sent to a sanatorium where it was thought to cure her of tuberculosis. One day her parents received a telegram; the postmaster had been ill and a boy had been taken on for the day to deliver the mail. Telegrams being unusual in small Polish towns they tore it open without checking the envelope'; (*but she knows it all by heart and has no need to refer to her notes*) 'he'd taken it to the wrong address. It had been meant for the apartment next door and by strange ill-fortune the telegram read, "Come at once your child is very ill." The child next door had been staying with relatives and died without seeing its parents. Wanda's parents packed at once but their speeding carriage was involved in an accident that proved fatal. These events hung like an accusative hand of God over her life.' What a life! And no one cared then and no one cares now. Not about your poetry nor my translations.

(*The* LIGHTS DIM *down.*

A banging on a wall is heard. It is BOOMY *calling for* EMANUEL's *attention.*)

BOOMY'S VOICE. Manny! You listening? 'I Kahelth, I the

preacher, was king over Israel and Jerusalem. And I gave my heart to seek and search out by wisdom concerning all things that are done under heaven; this sore travail hath God given to the sons of man to be exercised therewith. I have seen all the works that are done under the sun; and behold, all is vanity and vexation of spirit ...' Ecclesiastes.

(*A return of banging.*)

EMANUEL'S VOICE. Boomy! You listening? 'If the zaddick serves God', says Rabbi Nahman of Bratzlav, 'but does not take the trouble to teach the multitude, he will descend from his rung.' From Martin Buber.

Scene Four

The classroom. ROSA *enters with a chair and briefcase. She is a Ministry of Education careers-advisory officer, and is addressing a rowdy group of school-leavers from a tough neighbourhood. She's tentative, apologetic and finally ineffectual amid their assorted sighs and rasping sounds. It is her first confrontation.* (*Note: It is essential that* ROSA *does not appear to be addressing the audience.*)

ROSA. Now my task isn't easy, now is it? So some quiet, please. There are a lot of you boys and I don't know you each individually and so I can't really know what's the best job you're suited for and we need to talk about it. Nor is it only a matter of what *you're* suited for, is it? But what suits you. After all, I think insufficient attention is paid to what is likely to make us feel fulfilled. Society isn't very good at that yet, is it? It's a bit of a monster actually. Eats up everything, indiscriminately. (*Mocking laughter.*) And so, my task is all the more important and what I propose to do is outline the kinds of jobs that are open to you, roughly, very roughly you understand, and then for the next week I'll be available to speak to you individually. Those who want that is. Does that sound alright to you? (*Growing offensive noise.*) Does that sound like a good approach? Have you any suggestions for another method? I'd gladly listen. (*Pause, into which the sound swells.*) That's alright then. Good.

(*The noise is overwhelming.*)

Scene Five

SARAH's *council flat. At this moment she is bringing in food to another nephew,* RUDI, *tall, wild-eyed and bearded. He's a compulsive talker of half-finished, disjointed thoughts, constantly accompanied by gestures.*★

He is setting up an automatic slide-projector from which will be projected, throughout his talking and eating, slides of his gaudily coloured, tortured, primitive-type paintings.

SARAH (*from the kitchen*). You see the 'Succah'?
RUDI. I see it. She's become religious. A religious socialist!
SARAH. I'm doing it for your Aunt Gerda.
RUDI. *Two* mad aunts.
SARAH. I need some branches with leaves to cover it.
RUDI. So?
SARAH. So can you get some for me?
RUDI. Leaves? It's early autumn.
SARAH. We've got an Indian summer. There's still leaves.
RUDI. Leaves! Get leaves, she says. Where can I get leaves from? My garden? Who's got gardens these days? A

★ Rudi talks without full-stops or commas, but the text is sparsely punctuated in order to facilitate the actor's task and to save the reader from irritation.

room, a kitchen and a bathroom with three other people
that's what I've got. Can you grow trees in a bathroom?
Pot plants maybe, but not trees.

SARAH. Don't make jokes, Rudi.

RUDI. Jokes! Who's making jokes? What's funny about
anything?

SARAH. Rudi!

RUDI. Alright! I'll find you some leaves.
    (SARAH *enters with a tray of food.*)
    (*Referring to projector*) I'll show you.

SARAH. Eat!

RUDI. Forty-two pounds it cost, but this way a man can show
who he is, what he is and no doubts, you know what I
mean?

SARAH. The food'll get cold.

RUDI. In the garment factory they laugh. So! They laugh!
What's laughter?

SARAH. What you doing?

RUDI. A projector! Watch! Automatic and—no touching.
    (*Switches off room light, switches on machine; we receive
    the first shock of his 'work'. Satisfied, he sits to eat.*)
There! Photographs! You don't have photographs? No
one believes you. Saves a lot of talking, explaining. Like
this you show them, they can see, it's your work, your
name. I get tired talking, talking; lose breath, waste time,
you know what I mean? You want to see some of the
paintings? There's one in Hackney library and half a
dozen in a new Israeli restaurant, Stoke Newington end
of Northwold Road. Open ten in the morning till one,
two, maybe three in the morning, for three weeks. But
I'm not forcing you to go to not go you please yourself.
Who can force people? Force people you make enemies,
they get annoyed, they start lying—who can be bothered?
People always have excuses why they can't go—they're
busy, they've got appointments, they're ill—I never

knew people could be so ill so many times. You got commitments? I understand. What can I tell you? That you're my aunt? That you *must* go because you're family? So what? That's no reason. You please yourself. You go because you *want* to go, you're interested. You know what I mean? It won't stop me. Nothing stops me. I go on because I know if you don't go on for yourself you've had it; with jealousy from this one from that one, you wouldn't believe people can be so jealous, in every place, over everything, one person watching you, another one frightened in case you get more marks than them, you know what I mean? Like this I paint and I keep track where the paintings go. No one lets their work go somewhere without them knowing, you can be swindled, but me? I got photographs, with my name, on both sides, and it's proof and one day they'll sell and I'll earn money enough to take no notice of the lot of them. And they want me, you know that? To give my paintings. They chase me, write to me, the librarian, to bring, to hang. Because people, you know, they don't like reality, they hate reality, they're frightened. That's why there's all these goings on with revolutions and riots and violence. But it costs money—for paints, for hardboard, for framing. Me, I don't give them to frame anymore, I do my own the way I want them because one painting I gave and I said I wanted it in ten days' time and the girl wrote it down 'ten days' for Saturday but I went and nothing was done. 'The boys didn't know,' she said. They didn't know! They didn't *care*! They don't want to do any work, just to get paid while they flirt around, so it wasn't done and I took it away because who can wait while they mess things up for you? Everyone's busy messing things up for you. I could tell you stories. In every business. Twisting and dishonesty. One bloke says to me 'Take one of your paintings down and pretend you sold it, fool the people.'

But who can remember such things? This story, that story—how long can you go on doing that before you get found out—you know what I mean? Me, I can't work that way.

Now SCENE SIX *begins to merge into this scene. It is* MILLIE's *council flat.*
She's an old woman, tiny, withering, with a cracked voice. She potters aimlessly about the flat, her mind wandering.

MILLIE. And where are my brothers? I had brothers, where are they? A funny thing. They stay away. Who tells them to stay away?

RUDI. The other day I walked in the street and I found a wallet so I picked it up and I could see people watching me, waiting to see if I was gonna put it in my pocket. But I counted the notes, the pound notes and the pennies and all the receipts—packed with receipts, you could see she did the football pools—and I took it to the police-station and there there was forms, forms, you should see the forms, and every penny was counted and noted down and they told me if there was no claim in fourteen days they'd write to me. But she claimed and I got the letter with inside a postal order for ten shillings and it was worth everything to me, more than all the values.

MILLIE. No answer. No one makes an answer.

RUDI. Who understands art?

MILLIE. Terrible, terrible, terrible.

RUDI. People listen to other people, no one comes to see the work and then they want you to explain: 'what does it mean?'

MILLIE. Who am I talking to?

RUDI. What does it mean!

MILLIE. *I* don't know anymore.

RUDI. They don't *know* what it means?

MILLIE. I don't *know* anymore.

RUDI. They can't *see* what it means?

MILLIE. Ach! Leave me alone.

RUDI. It means what I understand!

MILLIE. I should worry! Brothers!

(*She finds herself by the phone. Dials.*)

RUDI. You know what I don't like doing? Portraits! A man can only show one kind of face when he's made to sit and think: sadness.

(*SARAH picks up phone.*)

MILLIE. Sarah?

SARAH. Who is it?

RUDI. One day someone asks me to paint Dayan.

MILLIE. It's Millie, Millie. Who else?

SARAH. You alright?

RUDI. Why Dayan?

MILLIE. I'm alright, but where are my brothers?

SARAH. What brothers?

RUDI. 'Paint Dayan please, it's a Jewish neighbourhood'!

MILLIE. My brothers. I had three brothers.

SARAH. Millie, your brothers are dead.

RUDI. So I said, 'How can I paint Dayan? I don't know him'!

SARAH. Millie?

RUDI. 'From a newspaper,' they said.

SARAH. Millie!

RUDI. A newspaper!

MILLIE. Dead?

RUDI. 'Give me a real live photograph,' I said, 'maybe I can do something.'

MILLIE. I know they're dead.

SARAH. Millie!

MILLIE. So, they're dead. And your husband?

SARAH. What are you talking about! My husband is also dead.

MILLIE. Also dead! Shoin!

SARAH. You know that, Millie.

MILLIE. Of course I know. I know everything. Terrible. Terrible.

(MILLIE *replaces receiver and sits looking about her.*)

SARAH. Millie!

MILLIE. So goodbye then.

(SARAH *dials back.*)

RUDI. The man in the restaurant asks me to paint his sign — I don't mind that I'm an artist and he asks me to paint his sign, but when it's only half done he says he can't get a ladder to finish the job. He *says*.

SARAH. Millie?

RUDI. But maybe it's not true.

MILLIE (*picking up receiver*). Who is it?

SARAH. She doesn't know me.

RUDI. Maybe he doesn't want to *pay* me.

SARAH. It's Sarah.

MILLIE. Sarah? How are you? I never hear from you.

RUDI. And maybe I won't ask to *be* paid.

SARAH. She's wandering.

RUDI. But all of a sudden he can't get a ladder.

SARAH. You just phoned me, you forgotten already?

MILLIE. Of course I'm alright.

SARAH. Millie, stop it! You musn't forget things.

MILLIE. Yes, yes, yes.

(MILLIE *replaces her receiver.*)

SARAH. Millie!

RUDI. So, the sign's only half done.

MILLIE. Funny woman, she is. So many years my brothers are dead and she doesn't remember.

(SARAH *has replaced her phone and sits, unhappy, uncertain.*)

RUDI. I tell you, two things I don't do: I don't jump into other people's business and I don't jump into other people's fights. Who knows what it's all about, you get caught up, *you're* the good one, and you get murdered! By mistake.

Scene Six

Now this scene comes fully into its own.
MILLIE *plugs in an electric kettle, puts tea in a strainer, prepares cup and saucer. Thinks. Climbs on a chair to reach for a pot on top of a cupboard. Inside are five-pound notes. She counts and throws them on the floor.*

MILLIE. Five pounds, ten, fifteen, twenty, twenty-five, thirty, thirty-five … (*Counts on in mumbles, scattering the notes like seeds*) … seventy-five, eighty, eighty-five, ninety. (*Stops. Looks. Long pause. Descends. Moves to pour water through tea-strainer. Adds milk. Looks back to money on floor.*)
It's good to have money.
(*Takes her tea and stands looking vacantly out by the window. Long silence.*)
My brothers. My poor brothers. Where are my poor brothers?

Scene Seven

Darkness. EMANUEL's *garden again. Again the light of dawn and again he comes from the hammock on the porch, howling.*
GERDA *follows to comfort him once more.*

GERDA. You'll kill me, Manny. I promise you, you'll bring me to an early grave.
EMANUEL. Night again! Always when no one can hear.
GERDA. For weeks now, night after night, for weeks.
EMANUEL. There must be something.
GERDA. Pills. Take pills. That's something.

EMANUEL. Perhaps in the morning—in all the newspapers, on the headlines, they'll say something.

GERDA. Stop it! You're trembling.

EMANUEL. On every headline in every newspaper, all over the world—something to reassure us.

GERDA. Not the world. Not the whole world. Can't I make you understand? No man can think about the whole world in his little brain. It's a little brain you've got, I've got, everyone's got. It'll crack, Manny, listen.

EMANUEL. Freedom! It's so important—it's got to be dictated.

GERDA. All my life.

EMANUEL. Justice? Force it!

GERDA. All the time we've been married you've never given yourself a moment's real happiness.

EMANUEL. Contradictions!

GERDA. You know that? All my time with you, not a moment's peace.

EMANUEL. Chaos and contradictions!

GERDA. And what are you?

EMANUEL. What's that for a life!

GERDA. A tailor! A little Jewish tailor!

EMANUEL. What's that for a life! Chaos and contradictions!
(She leads him back to the hammock and goes wearily into the house. He returns to sleep.
Morning and a slow, slow sunlight.
GERDA *brings him his usual breakfast of eggs, toast and china tea. A few hours have passed.)*

GERDA *(pouring)*. Pea water it looks like.

EMANUEL *(in rising from hammock, has small tussle with entangled blankets)*. It's started! I've woken up! Problems!

GERDA. You heard? They've landed on the moon.

EMANUEL. I'm very happy. The farther out they reach the more left behind I feel.

GERDA. You're trembling.

EMANUEL. I'm trembling! I'm trembling! I marvel, so I

tremble. The earth they leave is the ground that falls away from *me*. I didn't have an identity *before*? *Now* I've got nothing. (*Shudders.*) I should stop camping out at nights.

GERDA. Stop saying. Do!

EMANUEL. I'm too old to camp out.

GERDA. Who says you're too old?

EMANUEL. Look at that sky. I'm just getting used to the earth they give me the moon. I haven't enough problems? So, I marvel and I tremble. (*Reaches for book in hammock.*) Boomy! I need to have a go at my fraternal Doomsday Book.

GERDA. Manny!

EMANUEL. And have I got a quote!

GERDA. You know what I'd like to see? I'd like to see *you* two quarrel. Say two words of your own to each other.

EMANUEL. It starts my day.

GERDA. You've been having quarrels through other people's books for years now. Yell at him in your own voice for a change.

EMANUEL (*banging on wall*). Boomy? You listening? (*Struts and declaims in playful harangue*) ' … religious difference causes no trouble today … The Jew, the Catholic, the Greek, the Lutheran, the Calvinist, the Anabaptist, the Socinian, the Memnonist … ' The Socinian, the Memnonist? (*Shrugs.*) ' … The Socinian, the Memnonist, the Moravian, and so many others, live like brothers in these countries, and contribute alike to the good of the social body. They fear no longer in Holland that disputes about predestination will end in heads being cut off. They fear no longer at London that the quarrels of Presbyterians and Episcopalians about liturgies and surplices will lead to the death of a king on the scaffold … IT – WILL – NEVER – BE – REPEATED. Philosophy, the sister of religion, has disarmed the hands that superstition had so long stained with blood, and the human mind' (*approaching triumph now*) 'awakening from its intoxication is *amazed* at the excesses into which fanaticism had led it.' The undisputed crown-king of reason. VOL—TAIRE.

(*Silence.*)

What's he doing? (*Calling*) Did you hear it? You still think all can't be well with the world? (*To* GERDA) Is he awake?

GERDA. I took him his breakfast and he looked at the eggs and he said, 'Children who weep at the death of the first chicken they see killed laugh at the death of the second.' And he ate.

BOOMY'S VOICE. 'They who protested that all is well are Charlatans ... glance over the human race ... behold these battlefields, strewn by imbeciles with the corpses of other imbeciles. See these arms, these legs, these bloody brains, and all these scattered limbs; it is the fruit of a quarrel between two ignorant ministers (BOOMY *enters, book in hand, declaiming in a mock histrionic voice*) ... Enter the neighbouring hospital, where are gathered those who are not yet dead ... and then tell me all is well. Say the word if you dare ... over the ruins of a hundred towns that have been swallowed up by earthquakes ... And to complete this true and horrible picture, fancy yourself amid the floods and volcanoes that have so often devastated so many parts of the world; amid the leprosy and the plague that have swept it. And do you, who read this, recall all *you* have suffered, admit that evil exists, and do not add to so many miseries and horrors the wild absurdity of denying them.' (*Pause.*) Voltaire.

(*He has walked slowly round them and has gone with his last words.*

EMANUEL is upset. He brings his tailor's dummy from the room to the porch.)

EMANUEL. Work! Look! My hand doesn't shake. It can still cut cloth. My fingers are strong. I can still sew. Your son wants a suit? He shall have a suit. Your grandchildren want coats? They shall have coats. (*Pause.*) He should still have been reading Carlyle.

Scene Eight

The street. Evening. MARTIN, *Boomy's son, paces up and down.* BOOMY *appears.*

BOOMY. You couldn't come into the house? What's this! A clandestine meeting outside where I live!

MARTIN. I was arrested yesterday.

BOOMY. Come into the house, your aunt will make you some food.

MARTIN. I'm only out on bail.

BOOMY. You should leave politics alone.

MARTIN. I might get a prison sentence.

BOOMY. I've told you—it's the age of computers, the problems are different. Come inside.

MARTIN. I need some money.

BOOMY. A thick ear you need.

MARTIN (*exploding*). Take me seriously.

BOOMY. Secret meetings with my children I should take seriously?

MARTIN. A hundred pounds and you'll never see me again.

BOOMY. A hundred pounds for the pleasure of not seeing my son again? That's sense? That's an intelligent, responsible person talking?

MARTIN. *You're* a responsible person I suppose.

BOOMY. I've read too much! I've seen too much!

30

MARTIN. Well that's you, not me. Stop drowning me with your experience of men.

BOOMY. My quarrel is with God not men.

MARTIN. Good! You quarrel with God about important jobs—earthquakes, cyclones, droughts—I'll quarrel with men about trivialities—poverty, injustice, social orders— only lend me a hundred pounds, please.

BOOMY. I can't be expected to get excited about students' liberties.

MARTIN. There's a crisis.

BOOMY. There's always a crisis.

MARTIN. Yes! Always! That's how it must be in order for things to get better.

BOOMY. You mean like Stalin telling the German communists not to worry about Hitler, I suppose, because he'll create the right crisis for the German proletariat to take over? Madness! The worst things are, the worse they get! What did women do when they got the vote? Two world wars we've had.

MARTIN. One. Women got the vote in 1928.
(*They smile at one another.*)

BOOMY. You want freedom? Show me you can use it.
(*Sweetly said, but ill-chosen words. The quarrel slowly mounts again.*)

MARTIN. There's nothing I've ever done that you've made me feel proud of.

BOOMY. You want revolution? Show me your plans for the new world.

MARTIN. You made everything seem like an act of delinquency, and every time I listened, thinking you were maybe right.

BOOMY. You want to make people happy? Where's your wife, where's your child? Are they happy?

MARTIN. At no point have I behaved impetuously, no matter how much you've tried to make me think I have.

31

BOOMY. Have you learnt how to be a husband yet? A father? Show me these things.

MARTIN. But I'm not a delinquent and I'm not a fool, and I will, I will follow my conscience.

BOOMY. Show me these things, maybe I'll trust you.

MARTIN. I've STUDIED! I've studied and I've studied responsibly. I've thought and I've thought carefully. When I worked in the holidays didn't I share my earnings with the house? I do not like what I see. That's not unnatural and if doing what you disagree with is called irresponsible then irresponsible I am! (*Moves to go, turns back. Softly.*) You're the failure. A self-pitying, malicious failure and I won't believe in the image you've given me of myself. (*Leaves.*)

BOOMY (*calling after him*). 'That which is crooked cannot be made straight; and that which is wanting cannot be numbered ... For in much wisdom is much grief; and he that increaseth knowledge increaseth sorrow.' (*Pause.*) Ecclesiastes!

    BOOMY, *heartbroken, goes back into the house. The* LIGHTS DIM. *We hear a banging on the wall.*)

EMANUEL'S VOICE. Boomy! You listening? I'm reading from Martin Buber again. 'This is what Rabbi Leib, son of Sarah, used to say about those rabbis who expound the Torah: "What does it amount to—their expounding the Torah! A man should see to it that all his actions are a Torah and that he himself becomes so entirely a Torah that one can learn from his habits and his motions and his motionless clinging to God." '

Scene Nine

SARAH's *flat. She is watering her plants.*

A bell, like that of an old town-crier, is heard ringing to the accompaniment of a sing-song voice.

JACK'S VOICE. It's Jack-o-bell ringing, Jack-o-bell ringing. His warning he's ringing.

SARAH. Ah! Jack, Jack!

JACK'S VOICE. Don't come you near me, don't come you near me, the plague is upon me, the devil is in me.

(*Ringing continues, dying away at times as though he's walking backwards and forwards outside her door.*)

SARAH. I tell him. Does he listen? They'll take him away one day and he's not mad. (*She takes ingredients and materials from cupboard and prepares to bake a cake.*)

JACK'S VOICE. Jack is a-dying, the young folk is living, Jack is a-going, the young folk is coming. Don't come you near me, the plague is upon me, the devil is in me, the young folk is living.

(*Abrupt silence.*

SARAH goes to the door, leaves it open and returns to her baking.

After a long pause JACK stands by the door, struggles with himself but then comes in. He sits by her, an old cockney neighbour. Silence, then—)

SARAH. They'll take you away.

JACK. Do I care, Missus?

SARAH. Everyone on this new estate is old. You're not the only one.

JACK. I've lived a terrible life, Missus, wicked. Nothing you'd ever dream about.

SARAH. We've all been angels, I suppose.

JACK. Born a bastard, I was. Parents who didn't want me. Now wot abaht that? Ain't that a plague? A real, right plague that little fact is. Musn't contaminate people with that, Missus.

SARAH. Who do you think takes notice these days, silly man?

JACK. This silly man. All me life. Plagued me. And I beat me wife for it and drove me children from their own doorstep. Wot sort of a bloke's that?

(SARAH *takes glass and half-bottle of whisky from a cupboard. Pours him a tot.*)

SARAH. Don't tell anyone.

JACK (*drinks in one gulp*). Do you know, Missus, when I was in the war, in the jungle, I let a man die? A mate. Let 'im die. We was sent to round up snipers, a group of us, each with our little bit of ration, for three days. And this bloke, 'ee got it on the first day, in the side. The 'ole of 'is side out. And as I pass 'im 'ee calls, 'Got a drop o' water, mate? Just a drop.' And I looks at 'im and I thinks: 'ee's only got another hour or two in 'im, and me, I got another forty-eight hours to go. I need that water. And I leaves 'im. Now, Missus, wot sort of a bloke am I to leave a dying mate go thirsty, eh? A wicked life. Twenty-three years a rotten sergeant, bullying, foul-mouthed; nothing lovely abaht me at all. Contaminated!

(*Silence.*)

SARAH. I'm baking a cake for my daughter.

JACK. You're always doing something, Missus. Cooking, cleaning, watering plants, making us sign petitions. *I* never seen you still.

SARAH. You think *you're* wicked? I'll tell you a secret. You know one of my greatest pleasures? I'm ashamed to tell you, but listen. (*Pours another drink.*) To keep you company in wickedness, I'll confess. You've never met my son-in-law, have you? My daughter you've seen, she's got a job as a careers-advisory officer with the Ministry of Education, such a profession! She went to university, got degrees, honours and I-don't-know-what, but she couldn't decide on a profession for herself so she took up advising others. (*Pause.*) Still—her husband, you know what he does? I didn't think such a job existed but it does—he's a

34

soil expert. True! A soil expert! He looks at earth through a microscope to find out how to make things grow. A clever man. I'm not saying he's not a clever man. He works hard but—he's a climber. Imagine! won't even leave his wife in peace—thinks she ought to go into television or newspapers or make more degrees. I also think she ought to do something better, but I don't nag her and I don't care so much so long she's happy.

JACK. And is she happy, Missus?

SARAH. She's not happy, Missus. 'Missus!'—What's that for a name?

JACK. Can't call you Sarah, Missus. 'Missus' is polite, ain't it—Sarah?

(*Her smile is shy, his—cheeky.*)

Don't that deserve another drink?

SARAH. You're not mad.

JACK. Didn't say I was, just said I was wicked.

SARAH. I'm telling you a confession. This son-in-law of mine, in his house, is full with boxes with different soils. And all the time he's planting, planting, and cutting and mixing and adding things to the earth and—you know what? There's not a flower in the house! Can't make a thing grow. Boxes, that's all, with soil. Nothing grows. And it gives me such pleasure. Every time he comes here I make sure I've got a new plant or a new bud and I show him. 'What do you think?' I say. 'Big surprise! I did nothing to it and look—a new shoot!'

Scene Ten

A different class. ROSA *addresses them, with more firmness but still the wrong approach; still too reasonable, open to derision.*

ROSA. Alright, alright! So you make noises and send me up. But what's the point? Look, you've all got another sixty years to get through. I mean that's a long time, that needs thinking about. What you decide now can affect your whole life. I can't understand why you don't care about that. (*Noises of mock surprise.*) Listen, look at it this way. You're sixteen now. How many of you have friends of fourteen? You're different from them, aren't you? They're almost like kids to you. And at fourteen were you the same as you were at ten? And so, can't you imagine yourselves being different in the future? When you're twenty, twenty-five, thirty-five, fifty? Can't you imagine that you'll feel differently, think differently, have different needs? That's got to be prepared for, hasn't it? Can't you project yourselves forward, with your imagination? Can't you use your imagination to put yourselves into another situation? (*Noise.*) No, I don't suppose you can. I must be bloody mad.

(*Crescendo of noise, mock applause.*)

Scene Eleven

TERESSA's *room. She sits amid the chaos of her table, working on her translations.*

TERESSA (*reading from a sheet*).

> 'For Oh the wind like hammers hound
> And mock my life with warning sound;
> Those winds who for all others sing
> Prepare for me an inevitable ending.'

'Prepare for me' or 'prepare me for'? There's a difference. Or is there? Problems! Always the same question. Should

36

I translate the exact words or the exact meaning? The exact words would be: 'The winds sing for everyone else but I am to be prepared for they whisper "dying, dying".' The sense is poetic but the words aren't. Or are they? What about:

> 'Those winds who for all others sing
> Whisper to me of dying, dying.'

But then you lose her intention to show how the winds of life are preparing her for what she believes is the inevitable retribution of death. She feels guilty for her parents' death and she sees all life as her trial. Suppose we say:

> 'Those winds who for all others sing
> Prepare my death with whispering.'

But then you see, Teressa darling, she repeats the words 'dying, dying' so that it also *sounds* like the wind. You'll lose all that. Well, something is always lost I suppose. I wonder, would it matter if I made it a verse of five lines instead of four?

> 'Prepare me for my death.
> With their whispering, whispering.'

So:

> 'For Oh the winds like hammers hound
> And mock my life with warning sound;
> Those winds who for all others sing
> Prepare me for my death
> With their whispering, whispering.'

God knows! Enough now. You've been working on that verse for two months now. Leave it alone. Come back to it next week. (*Pushes papers aside.*) Now what should I do?

Scene Twelve

The street. Afternoon. MILLIE, *wandering, humming, sometimes backing away from what she peers at, surprised, finally walking round in circles.*

MILLIE. Sarah? Is that you? Have you moved? You used to live near here, somewhere. (*Nods and hums to imaginary passers-by.*) Good afternoon, good afternoon.

> (THREE YOUTHS *approach and begin to mimic her distress. She peers at them as though she doesn't see or understand their presence.*
>
> TERESSA *appears, on her way to Sarah's. The* YOUTHS *depart.*)

TERESSA. Is that you, Millie?

MILLIE (*peering at her*). Sarah?

TERESSA. It's me, darling, Teressa. You going to Sarah's?

MILLIE. I'm not going to Sarah's. Why should I be going to Sarah's? She got a tea or something? Sarah always has a tea, with people, always full with people.

TERESSA. Were you out for a walk?

MILLIE. Where does she find them, so many people?

TERESSA. Were you lost?

MILLIE. Lost? Me? I was going to the shops, to buy bread, a little chicken and — things. I got to shop, can't stop shopping.

TERESSA. Come, Millie. I'm going to Sarah's, come with me.

MILLIE. Funny thing. I was also going to the same place.

> (*Moves in the wrong direction.* TERESSA *guides her back.*)

TERESSA. This way, Millie.

MILLIE. This way? She moved? I didn't know Sarah moved. She tells me nothing, all these years, she's supposed to be my friend, nothing.

Scene Thirteen

SARAH's *flat.* JACK *is hanging things on the 'Succah'.*
SARAH *reads a letter.*

JACK. It wobbles.

SARAH. I know it wobbles.

> (TERESSA *and* MILLIE *knock at door.*
> JACK *stands up, alarmed, backs to the wall.*)

JACK. Tell them to stay away. Wait till I've gone out. Not
contaminating no one, I'm not.

SARAH (*at door*). It's only Millie and Teressa.

TERESSA. She was wandering, you know that? Lost. Good
afternoon, Jack.

JACK. 'Afternoon, Missus.

SARAH (*to* MILLIE). It's Jack. You remember Jack, my
neighbour?

MILLIE. Jack? Jack? I don't know no Jack.

SARAH. You must remember, Millie. Think!

MILLIE (*one isn't certain if she's pretending*). Jack? Jack?

SARAH. On about half a dozen occasions. (*Pause.*) You *must*
remember. It's *not* too much for you to forget. You've
seen him here, in this very room — and always by the wall.
Come away from the wall, Jack, and stop being a silly
man. I'm surrounded by silly people. Millie, you mustn't
forget things. Teressa, make tea please. (*Back to* MILLIE)
You mustn't forget! Make your mind think, think!
Forget things and you'll go to pieces. Look at her, as if
she doesn't hear me. Sit, both of you.

> (MILLIE *wanders over to the window to gaze out.* JACK
> *remains glued to the wall.*)

Ach! I should care. (*Returns to preparations.*)

TERESSA'S VOICE (*from the kitchen*). Three young thugs were
teasing her. God knows what would have happened if I
hadn't come. (*Pause.*) The sons of your working-class.

SARAH (*calling back*). Leave me alone with 'your' working-class. *My* working-class! She's always on to me. Look! (*Picks up a letter.*) A letter from my brother in Lithuania! Someone had to bring it to my door, how do you think it got here? Carrier pigeon? You're making tea, you've got milk, every morning there's a pint of milk at my door. Who brings it? Prince Philip? And who do you think got it from the cow? His wife? Look! (*Switches light on and off.*) Light! How did it get here? (*Moves to telephone.*) You want to speak to your sister in America? Speak! Turn this, wait a little, a voice answers. Who's putting you through? Who does it? Everywhere you look—new buildings, new roads, new cities—who puts them there? So leave me alone about my working-class. (*Continues baking.*) That's shut her up.

TERESSA (*from the kitchen*). Nothing shuts me up, I must warn you. You know what they say: those near the grave have nothing to lose but their life. A very funny saying, I've always thought, but it means something. Me, I've never had much to lose anyway, so I've always talked. Why shut up? People close their ears anyway so it's necessary to keep talking or you'd forget language. Very important, language. Without language men think with their fists.

SARAH. You see, she's contradictions. Half her pension she sends to left-wing charities. Can't make up her mind which side she's on.

TERESSA (*from the kitchen*). I know which side I'm on, but who says everyone that's on my side I should like? Jack, you owe me ten shillings.

(JACK *is staring uncertainly at* MILLIE, *she fascinates him. Then, to her*—)

JACK. You know wot they do with the foreskin of Jewish babies, Missus?

SARAH. Jokes like that aren't nice, Jack.

JACK. Send them to Israel to plant under trees.

SARAH. She won't understand.

JACK. Forest upon forest. Honest! And that's wot makes the trees grow straight.

SARAH. You're a crude man.

JACK. I'm making her laugh.

(MILLIE *is ignoring him.*)

SARAH. She's laughing, look!

JACK. I'm wicked, always was and always will be.

(TERESSA *enters with a tray of tea and biscuits.*)

It's here.

TERESSA. What's where?

JACK. The ten shillings. Up me leg.

TERESSA. Did he say 'leg'?

JACK. Pull up me trouser-leg.

TERESSA. *I* should pull up your trouser-leg?

JACK. You ain't never met a man wot's mean like me. Can't bear to part with nothing. Me 'ands won't bring themselves to part with a thing. You wants it, you 'as to take it.

(*Amazed.* TERESSA *moves to raise his trouser-leg.*)

A handkerchief. See it? Tied round me calf. In there.

(*She unties a handkerchief that's attached to his leg.*)

Should be two pound-notes and some silver. Take it, 'cos I can't give it.

(*She extracts some coins and puts the handkerchief back in his hands. He ties it back.*)

Can't believe it, can yers? I told you, Missus. I'm wicked. A man born a bastard remains one, and all your fighting 'gainst it won't help. (*Picks up bell, leaves ringing.*) Jack's a-dying, the young folk is living, Jack's a-going, the young folk is coming.

SARAH. Your tea!

(*Door slams. We hear* JACK *from outside ringing and chanting.*)

JACK'S VOICE. Don't come you near me, the plague is upon me, the devil is in me, the young folk is living.

EMANUEL'S VOICE. 'All things are literally better, lovelier, and more beloved for the imperfections which have been divinely appointed, that the law of human life may be Effort, and the law of human judgment, Mercy.' John Ruskin.

Scene Fourteen

BOOMY's *room. It is filled with books and the bits and pieces of a large children's computer set.*
BOOMY *sits morosely.* GERDA *is by him.*

GERDA. I'm waiting for an answer. (*Pause.*) I've got to live between two brothers always quarrelling?

BOOMY. I was eight when our father brought us over.

GERDA. You were nine, you've forgotten. You were nine, Manny was ten, Sarah was twelve. So?

BOOMY. Did you know our father was rich?

GERDA. Comfortable, yes. Rich, no. But that he wasn't careful, *that* I know.

BOOMY. He was rich *and* he was careful. Before leaving Lithuania he converted his money into diamonds and gave them to a Gentile friend to take to Amsterdam; and from there, every year, his friend brought a few in for him. And slowly he built up a business in Black Lion Yard off the Whitechapel Road. One day – a robbery! An ordinary common-or-garden robbery and our father, bless him, for all that he was wise and careful, was not insured. Still, it was not the end of the world. There was one last bag expected from Amsterdam and those, our father said, were for us, to pay for our education. He was a frugal man, needed very little – his sons would provide. And to

Manny, because he came first, he gave the little bag of diamonds.

GERDA. Of this I knew nothing.

BOOMY. Wait, there's more you don't know. Did you know Manny was one of the first members of the Communist Party?

GERDA. Communist! Communist! He keeps saying he's a Communist, he refuses to join any of the groups and he quarrels with everybody.

BOOMY. But in those days he joined. A founder member. And you know what happened?

GERDA. O-my-God-no-he-gave-them-to-the-party-funds.

BOOMY. Ah! Gerda. I knew you'd think that. And so would every sane-minded person have thought it; and if he'd done that I think I'd have understood better—I might even have been proud. But no, that's not what happened. One day he says to me—I was sixteen at the time, the father dead, school finished, we were planning university —and Manny says to me: 'Boomy, come for a walk, let's see London, how much of London do we know?' So we walked, through Spitalfields to Liverpool Street, down through the city to Mansion House and out along the embankment to Westminster. What a walk that was, exhilarating! And we stood on the bridge and talked and talked about the future. How I was going to study medicine and he was going to study economics, perhaps go into Parliament—young men's talk, brave, happy. You ever stood on that bridge and looked at London? Wordsworth wrote a poem from it, the river bends, a wide sweep, you can look up and look down—beautiful! (Pause.) And we talked. (Pause.) And suddenly Manny says: 'But Boomy,' he says, 'everything we do must come from our own hands. You agree?' And of course I agree, 'cos I thought he was only talking about the efforts we would have to make in our studies. 'Good,' he says, and he embraces me and we cry and before I know it he's thrown the bag of diamonds into the river. (*Pause.*) You're paralysed, aren't you, Gerda? Can you imagine what *I* felt? I nearly choked him, on the spot. 'Little lunatic,' I yelled at him, 'lunatic!' And he kept saying 'but you agreed, you agreed' until I had to run away and he kept shouting after me, 'You agreed!' Agreed!

(*Long silence.* BOOMY *fiddles with the computer set. Tidies up a little.*)

GERDA. Give each other a little peace.

BOOMY. It's so bad, eh? I thought the worst was over. We don't scream like we used to. It's only a ritual that's left. Funny, even.

GERDA. But no friendship. Forgive him. You're both old now.

BOOMY. I'm not very good at being old. Some people are like that; only a certain period in their life suits them. Some are lovely children and rotten adults. Me, I was good at being young, not because I enjoyed it so much— I couldn't stop being bitter—but because I had strength, I could fight. That's my weakness, I can't bear being defenceless. You know things? Defence! You got a profession? Defence! You can talk? Defence! Instead? Tailors! Little schneiders. And now look at me, playing with children's computer sets in order to start understanding things. Now! Sixty-eight years old. Like a senile Doctor Faustus. You noticed that about our family? Look at our nieces and nephews: Rosa, trying to knock awareness into young people; Rudi, all his savings on night classes, psychiatry, engineering, singing and now—a painter. Dabbling! My brother has made of me, of our children, of himself—a dabbler. Even Martin, my son. A revolutionary! From love? No! from hate. Hatred of me. One thing leads to another!

(GERDA *leaves. Sound of banging on the wall.*)

EMANUEL'S VOICE. 'Cast off all superstition, and be more humane. But when you speak against fanaticism, anger not the fanatics; they are delirious invalids, who would assault their physicians. Let us make their ways more gentle, not aggravate them. And let us instil, drop by drop, into their souls that divine balm of tolerance which they would reject with horror if offered to them in full.' Voltaire.

Scene Fifteen

The street. GERDA *is on her way to shop.*
The THREE YOUTHS *approach and begin to mimic her limp.*
She is not afraid but retraces her steps. They continue to follow and mimic till she turns to face them.

GERDA. Silly boys. What do you want? To mimic me? Mimic then, it'll help you be thankful you've got strong legs.
(*One* YOUTH *does a specially cruel and grotesque imitation for the amusement of his companions.*)
Good! You feel better? Then let me pass.
(*They menace her.*)
You want to frighten me? I'm too old to be frightened, go home.
(*They limp round her in a circle.*)
It's really *me* you want to bash? Little bash-boys? *I'm* the biggest thing you can find? Look at me. Look at yourselves. Three of you. That's brave? I'm the biggest conquest you can make? Go home. Brave boys, go home!
(*Her reason intimidates them. Both sides watch each other. She seems to have won and leaves them.*
Alone there is nothing to feed their valour. One tries to revive the rest by another imitation. It fails. He does it again, more

violently. It begins to work. A third time he does it, stamping around as though beating a signal for attack. The other two pick it up and go off with their loud limping mockery. Silence. A scream.

JACK *walks by clanging his bell.*)

JACK. Jack-o-bell ringing, his warning he's ringing, the plague is upon me, the young folk is living, Jack is a-dying, the young folk is coming, the devil is in me, the young folk is living.

END OF ACT ONE

ACT TWO

Scene One

SARAH's *flat. Chairs on table.* SARAH *is cleaning up.** BOOMY *is with her.*

BOOMY. And he didn't even go to the police. 'Youth makes mistakes,' he says. Mistakes! His wife gets beaten up and he calls it high spirits. You know your brother's trouble?

SARAH. *My* brother and *your* brother.

BOOMY. You know our brother's trouble? He doesn't understand evil. He can't come to terms with the existence of evil. He's always looking for explanations. Some people are colour blind — he's evil blind.

SARAH. It could have been worse.

BOOMY. Can you imagine it? A mind so simple that it has to find reasons for everything, and because of that he doesn't act.

SARAH. A few bruises, that's all.

BOOMY. If *he* was confronted with a man about to strike him he wouldn't react like an ordinary man. He wouldn't raise his hand, reach out to grab something, hit back. No! He'd be paralysed by principles and by trying to work out why it was happening and in the meantime he'd be killed.

SARAH. She's strong, she'll survive.

BOOMY. Principles he's got!

SARAH. In a few days she'll be up and about but in the meanwhile they'll both stay with me. It'll be a pleasant change. Company. You want to stay also?

---

* From here on, preparations need to be made for the dinner. *What* happens *when* is best worked out by the director.

47

BOOMY. Principles! The trouble with principles is they make you take a stand about the *one* situation you know you're defeated in.

SARAH. I tell you something? I'm glad it happened. She'll be more careful next time.

BOOMY. And you can't talk your way out of it.

SARAH. Like this she's learnt and it won't happen again and with luck she'll live to be a year older.

BOOMY. Why can't you talk your way out of it? Because your intelligence tells you the situation is created by idiots or dogmatists or fanatics or psychopaths.

SARAH. Instead of talking, help!

(*He helps.*)

BOOMY. You're trapped! between your intelligence and your principles — you're trapped!

SARAH. Did I tell you the fright I had the other day?

BOOMY. Principles! Everyone has principles.

SARAH. I phoned Rosa and there was one of those recorded voices at the other end — she'd made a tape. A little speech! You know what it said? 'This is a recording. Mrs Rosa Luxemburg is dead. If you have any messages speak now and we'll do our best.'

BOOMY. The trouble is everyone imagines he's going to have to defend his principles in a romantic situation, where right will prevail.

SARAH. My daughter!

BOOMY. Beautiful!

SARAH. A joker!

BOOMY. But most situations are sordid, confused. Created by morons who *have* no principles — and there you are!

SARAH. We'll have a nice supper.

BOOMY. Caught!

SARAH. They're all coming.

BOOMY. You know what I think about principles?

SARAH. The first 'Succah' the children have ever had.

BOOMY. Principles are like loves and friendships — precious, special. You should only apply them where they're deserved, sparingly.

SARAH. Get hold of the end of the table.

(*He helps. Or, if other preparations have been decided upon, he helps with those.*)

BOOMY. And don't tell me a principle's a principle and that the nature of a principle is that it should be applied in all situations or else it's not a principle. That's the argument dishonest men give you in order to undermine you.

SARAH. I'm making chopped liver —

BOOMY. That's why men of principle are vulnerable —

SARAH. — strudel —

BOOMY. — they can always be defeated.

SARAH. — you'll see!

BOOMY. You want to be principled? Then make a principle of using your scruples only in an emergency, when they're *most* needed, when everyone else can understand them.

SARAH. You think there'll be enough room?

BOOMY. She should have screamed.

SARAH. That's the trouble with this flat, it's too small.

BOOMY. Straight away — she should have screamed. 'Help!'

SARAH. I keep telling Rosa 'Thank you for getting it but it's too small.'

BOOMY. 'Help! Help!' So everyone could have heard. 'Help!'

Scene Two

TERESSA's *flat.*

TERESSA. Perhaps if I do physical things I won't feel so lonely.

(*Her flat is a shambles. She begins pulling clothes off here and there stuffing them away.*)

Work! they say. Keep your body working! As if growing old you can do all the things you could when you were young.

(*But on bending she strains herself.*)

Aaah!

Work! they say. Give me a new body—I'll work!

(*She moves to a cupboard lined with medicine bottles. From one she takes a pill.*)

So! And that's for my lumbago. And what shall I take for the pain behind my ears, and my weak bladder, and my coughing fits and the pain in my chest and my fear? Fear! Who's got pills against fear?

(*On the table are a box of dominoes. She builds with them.*)

You know, darling, when a person *really* feels lonely? Not when they're alone and no one comes to see them—in such a case you can go out to people, even if they don't ask. No, it's when they don't have in their heart one little bit of a wish themselves to see other people. It's *not* having appetites for contact, that! That, my darling, makes for real loneliness. You, you're lucky, you're *not* lonely—you *want* contact. But who? That's your problem. And where? And when? (*Pause.*) And why? I always forget why. Such a memory! My memory is so bad that when I went to a psychiatrist to get it seen to I'd forgot why I came. (*Pause.*) No! That's not true. It's funny but it's not true. Who can afford a psychiatrist? Jokes! Even jokes I have to tell myself, and *that's* not funny, darling. My poor darling.

(LIGHTS DIM. *There is a banging on a wall.*)

BOOMY'S VOICE. 'Man is not what one calls a happy animal.' Carlyle.

Scene Three

SARAH's *council flat.* MARTIN *is knocking more nails into the* '*Succah*', *ineffectively trying to strengthen it.*

MARTIN. I'm afraid it'll always wobble.

SARAH. Let it. So will I always wobble.

(RUDI *enters carrying a bundle of branches tied with string.*)

RUDI. Trees! Get trees, she says. Where can I get trees from? My garden? Who's got a garden? One room and a kitchen I've got, with a bathroom for three other tenants to use — and their friends. I'm lucky if I get a bath once a week. (*Sees* MARTIN.) It's Martin?

MARTIN. Hello, Rudi.

RUDI. After all these years it's Martin.

MARTIN (*helping to untie bundle*). And where *did* you get them from?

RUDI. Can you grow trees in a bathroom?

SARAH. They're just right.

RUDI. Little pot plants, maybe. But trees?

(*They begin to lay them over the 'Succah'.*)

And how's my student? So many years you've been a student. When does a student stop being a student?

MARTIN. It's too long, isn't it?

RUDI. Who says it's too long?

MARTIN. You're right.

RUDI. I'm just asking.

MARTIN. It *is* too long.

SARAH. It's never too long to study. Study. You won't be sorry.

RUDI. You want to know where I got them? In the place where I go to evening classes they've got a big oak tree. Two in fact. I asked the caretaker. A few coppers, you know, on the side. Everything costs a few coppers. And he cut some for me. It needs pruning, he says. Pruning! And if it didn't need pruning? He'd still cut them! For coppers! Everything's possible for coppers.

MARTIN. Be careful how you lay them. It wobbles.

RUDI. Everything wobbles. You seen a piece of furniture these days that doesn't wobble.

SARAH. Study. Great learning. It's an honour.

RUDI. You know I go to evening classes?

MARTIN. I know. To study singing.

RUDI. That was last year. You see how long I don't see people in this family? A cousin! and he still thinks I'm singing.

MARTIN. What is it then?

RUDI. Painting. I paint. Oils, watercolours, gouache. You know what I mean?

SARAH. Study! It's a blessing to know things. My father was always telling me. Knowledge is light, ignorance is darkness.

Scene Four

MILLIE's *flat.* JACK *is with her. She gazes, as always, out of the window.*

JACK. No, Missus, I ses to meself, that lady can't be mad. Wot, that little frail thing? I seen women frail like that before but they outlive their men they did. Little things they were, pellets of steel. Pellets like them don't go mad, I ses to meself, and there's one of 'em. (*Waits for response. None comes.*) So I comes, leaves me bell behind and looks her up. She'll give me a cup of charley, I ses, and talk a little, an' the day'll pass and be the better for it. (*Still no reaction.*) Wot should I do? Stay at home? Ring me bell? You think a man don't tire of his own bell-ringing? So 'ere 'ee is, your Jack-o-bell. Tea I got, your good company and homemade bread pudding into the bargain.

MILLIE. My daughters were evacuated to Wales, you know. In the war. Five daughters I had. My poor husband! No son! And three were big. Big girls—worked in armaments. But the youngest? A place called Tredegar, in a little stone cottage, no electricity, no water, no nothing, miles from anywhere. My poor children. And this woman— you talk about madness?—this woman made them do strange things every night. One night combing her hair, another night rubbing her back, then washing her feet— funny woman. Who knows where your children go in war-time, eh? And *she* ended up in a home, my daughter told me, she went back one day and found her, in a room, padded, her hair sticking out like a tree, and my daughter said, 'You remember me?' and she did. For a second, she called her name, Becky, and then she forgot. Strange, yes? The whole place was strange. In the school the teacher used to tell them 'Because you're Jewish your nose will get longer and horns will come out of your head!' My poor girls. They believed him. Did you ever see? Horns! And each night they used to look in the mirror and it was true. They were growing girls and their noses got bigger! And all the time they were waiting for the horns. And all the time this woman, this mad woman, kept saying, 'Maybe your horns won't grow, maybe because you're in Wales they won't grow!' But the teacher kept saying, 'They must! They must!' Is that a teacher I ask you? And one day they came home for a holiday and my husband, God rest him, could see they were unhappy so he asks them, 'What's the matter?' And they told him and he says, 'Silly girls, look at me, your father, have *I* got horns?' And they looked and he was right, they could see, no horns!

(*Pause.*)

JACK. Yes, Missus, I ses to meself, you'll get a cup o' tea, a bit o' company and the day'll be the better for it.

(LIGHTS DIM. *A sound of banging on the wall.*)

EMANUEL'S VOICE. Boomy? You listening? 'Hast thou considered how each man's heart is so tremulously responsive to the hearts of all men; hast thou noted how omnipotent is the very sound of many men? ... Great is the combined voice of men; the utterance of their *instincts*, which are truer than their *thoughts*: it is the greatest a man encounters among the sounds and shadows which make up this World of Time.' Carlyle.

Scene Five

SARAH's *flat. A depressed* ROSA.

SARAH. You shouldn't let it upset you.

ROSA. I just can't break through to them.

SARAH. You'll try again.

ROSA. The problem's so immense.

SARAH. With another lot—you'll learn.

ROSA. And they can see, those little monsters, even before I begin, that I'm defeated. And wham! they step in.

SARAH. Who knows about things in the beginning?

(ROSA *kisses her mother.*)

ROSA. One day, Sarah, we will die.

SARAH. You, silly girl? *You're* at the age when you'll never die.

ROSA. It's the most terrible fact I know. Every lovely, lovely thing I cherish will, for me, one day, be ended. And I don't know when it will be, or how, or where. I try to think of it, imagine the circumstances, but I can't, there are too many possibilities. And it's such a pain, that loss,

of you—and me. You can't imagine how much I dread it.
Says Boswell: 'But is not the fear of death natural to man?'
Says Johnson: 'So much so, Sir, that the whole of life is
but keeping away the thoughts of it.' (*Pause.*) I won't ever
die happily; no matter what splendid life I lead I can't see
myself smiling sweetly with my last breath; I'll rage—
that's for sure. But could I rage less? What could I do to
make me rage less? I don't know. I ask myself but I don't
know. I can't even formulate the right questions. Capital
versus labour? Computer versus individual? Rich world
versus third world? Affluence versus spiritual poverty?
Which is it? One or all or something else? And if I find
out, what can I do? And those cruel little cripples—who'll
be the real victims, you know—they block me.

(SARAH *breaks away from her and throws a big white table-
cloth over the extended table.*)

SARAH. A white cloth!

(ROSA, *her mood spent, takes the other end.*)

Nothing like a white cloth, fresh, clean, happy.

ROSA. Happy! Happeeee!

(ROSA *now begins unpacking a box of drinks.*)

SARAH. What you doing?

ROSA. Drinks! I've bought you a little arsenal of socializing
equipment. All those thirsty tipplers you entertain.

SARAH. Take it back.

ROSA. It's a present. I got an income-tax rebate.

SARAH. You've got money? Keep it! You may need it one
day.

ROSA. Cointreau, gin, Tia Maria, cherry brandy, brandy—
only half-bottles. Indulge yourself.

SARAH. It makes me ashamed. Me, an old-age pensioner in a
block of flats for old-age pensioners.

ROSA. A *few* bottles.

SARAH. It's immoral. A couple of pounds they've got to live
on and I've got a brewery inside here.

ROSA. I love to see full cupboards. Got it from you. I used to love unpacking *your* shopping-bags. When I go shopping it's terrible, I can't stop. Biscuits from one shelf, tins from another, and cheeses—all those diffcrent cheeses. You never know who's coming. And I feel so ashamed. The children see me, taking, taking, taking—in a fever. What will they grow into, I think? (*Pause.*) I'll hide them under the bed.

SARAH. You're a good daughter, not everyone's got good daughters, take them back.

ROSA. Mother, there's not a law against having good daughters.

SARAH. You mean well, I'm very grateful, don't argue with me and take them back.

ROSA. There's no logic in you.

SARAH. She's starting on me again. Something else wrong with me.

ROSA. I'm not starting on you, I'm criticizing you.

SARAH. You're always criticizing me.

ROSA. No, *you're* always criticizing *me*.

SARAH. There! Another thing wrong I've done. I made a new year's resolution—no more quarrelling with the children.

ROSA. Will you stop being paranoic.

SARAH. Don't be crude.

ROSA. I'm not really criticising you. How could I? Everything *you* are, *I* am.

SARAH. Calling me names.

(ROSA *stops her in her work and embraces her from behind.*)

ROSA. Everything! The little I respect in myself I've inherited from you.

SARAH. A terrible life I gave you.

ROSA. You! Generosity, tolerance, intolerance, sanity, insanity. You!

SARAH. Leaving you alone to go out to work.

ROSA. The weather gets overcast—I'm depressed! You!

SARAH. Not caring enough for your education.

ROSA. When I lose my temper confronted with bloody-mindedness? You!

SARAH. You think it pleases me that you've inherited my faults?

ROSA. I read about the terrible things men do to each other— wars for gain or prestige, massacres for religious principles, cruelty to children, indifference to poverty—and then, one morning, one person, one, does something beautiful and I say, 'See! people *are* good!' You!

SARAH. *I* was a fool? I brought *you* up to be a fool.

ROSA. The pompous action that makes me giggle? You! My laughter, my ups, my downs, my patience, my impatience, my love of music, mountains, flowers, knowledge—a reverence for all things living? You! You, you, you!

Scene Six

The street. JACK *and* MILLIE.

JACK. Come, Missus, tonight's the night. With a hop, skip and a jump. Look!

(*There's a children's chalked game on the ground.* JACK *hops through it.*)

You do it, Missus.

MILLIE. You're a very funny man.

JACK. Too late for lying, Missus, too old to pretend. I rings me bell, they can go to hell.

MILLIE. A poet he is.

JACK. Quite right, little missus, little pellet of steel. A poet! With a hop and a skip and a jump.

(*Hops through the game once more and turns to face her.*)

Hated the army, hated the war, hated employers and all

their sweet smiles; and I learned that a man's got ter give 'is warning and cry stinking fish sometimes. But—I loves London and I loves England and I loves the little foreigners like you wot they let in to mix the blood a bit. Come, Missus, me arm. I'll escort you safe and sound to the other little Jewish lady wots my neighbour.

(*She takes his arm, shyly.*)

And wot a neighbour she is, she is. A fighter, a real little pellet of steel she is. Pellets of steel all you lot are. Come.

(*They walk on.*)

Scene Seven

SARAH's *flat. A restless* MARTIN.

SARAH. If I had a hundred pounds, I'd give you. Stay for a Friday-night supper and see your father.

MARTIN. I can't face him anymore, Sarah.

SARAH. A lonely, old man. What harm can he do you?

MARTIN. He thinks he's tough, but he's gloomy.

SARAH. You've got a court case hanging over you. Speak to him.

MARTIN. I try. I always try. 'Leave politics alone!' He screams at me.

SARAH. Prison. It might mean prison.

MARTIN. All that tough gloominess? It's soft really. And the softer he becomes, the harder I must be.

SARAH. Idiot's logic.

MARTIN. I look at him and I see myself. That softness? I'll catch it from him and it'll destroy me.

SARAH. You think you're not already? Your studies, your wife, your family—abandoned! That's not destruction?

MARTIN. It only looks like it.

SARAH. I'm losing patience.

MARTIN. They're leaving us no alternatives.

SARAH. They! They! Always someone else. And you think you're not doing just what *they* want? Window smashing, burning, insulting—everyone and anyone—little gestures?

MARTIN. They arrested a friend, Sarah; a sweet, frail young man. For months I'd been talking to him; arguing, explaining, making him read different books, giving him courage. He took nothing I said without checking, without counter-argument, without asking others. I worked so hard to persuade him that I grew to love him. He had the reddest hair I'd ever seen, was brilliant—much more than me—and diabetic. And when they arrested him they took one look at his long red hair and refused to *believe* he was diabetic. He died.

SARAH. An exception!

MARTIN. I wish it were.

SARAH. You can't make policies from exceptions.

MARTIN. I could tell you more.

SARAH. You can't tell me anything will excuse these actions.

MARTIN. Now *I'm* losing patience.

SARAH. If your family rots, your beliefs will rot.

MARTIN. I don't know what you want from us. You *taught* us to respect human beings, didn't you? To revere knowledge and despise gain? You and Uncle Manny? Well, didn't you? 'If a man is hungry while you eat you won't have peace,' you said. 'When you see injustice, protest!' Manny used to pack me off to school saying, 'Don't fight and don't let misery stop you laughing, but if you see a bully—stand up! Always stand up and be counted!' And he'd tell me, 'Take no notice of your father, he's a good man but he doesn't like himself.'

SARAH. So! your father's *made* mistakes.

MARTIN. Mistakes?

SARAH. Alright! He was wrong. Not right-minded with a

few natural mistakes—but wrong! From start to finish, wrong! What must you do? Scream insults at his old age? Spit on him? That's lovely? You shriek untenderly at him that he had no tenderness? You handle him violently for his violence upon you? That's inspiration? Leadership? You must have strength to ignore Boomy's weaknesses and leave him a little bit of useless old peace. What do you imagine *your* children will say at the sight of such ugliness in protest against ugliness? What must they learn from such a spectacle of your revenge? That's what you build new worlds with? What's this for revolution? Lovely! Oh, very lovely! Lovely, lovely, yes!

MARTIN. Do you think I enjoy the conscience you all gave me?

SARAH. Stay and speak with your father.

(*He leaves.*)

Scene Eight

Another class. ROSA *enters. She is determined to control them and does.*

ROSA. I'm here once and once only. And when I'm gone I'll not care one bit about any of you but you're going to care about and remember me. You, each one of you, are nothing in this society. Nothing! You are poor, used, nothings who will mostly end up unhappy, frustrated and thoroughly defeated. You *think* you're in control, that no one can shove you around, that you're God almighty free Englishmen but you're not. You can bash each other and pinch sweets and knock old women on the head but the great world goes on and ignores you or knows and cares little for you just as you boast that you know and care little for it. What, what is there you can do? Can you take a yacht round the world? Can you fly to wherever you want? Can you speak another language, split an atom, transplant a heart, live where you like, climb a mountain? You won't even find the job you want, most of you. So get that straight, firm, in your heads. It's a big world in which control rests with other people, not *you*. *Not* you. (*Pause.*) Good. You're listening. It makes a change. I don't say any of these things happily. I don't approve of this system I speak about and, in my own way, I fight it. I only tell you of it in the hope of stirring you to the challenge. I don't believe most of you will rise to it but that's not my concern just now. My concern is with the one boy among you who might benefit from my talk and have done with his tiny ambitions of petty kingships; the boy who *might* turn in on himself and find his real strengths. And it will *only* be one of you — the rest will end up on the scrap-heap of dead-end jobs with dead-eyed wives. (*Pause.*) You hate me, don't you? I can see from your eyes and clenched mouths that you hate every part of me; the sound of my voice, what I say, the way I dress, the life you imagine I lead. I'm sorry about that. Hate's a sterile emotion. Useless! It'll take you round in circles while others go straight for what they want. Still, I suppose that's the diet most of you will live with from now on. Hate. Sad. BUT HERE! Here is a book. Books! Take them. Use them. Other men may build a world out there you never dreamed of. Defend yourself! Books! Centuries of other people's knowledge, experience. Add it to yours, measure it with yours. They're your only key to freedom and happiness. Books! There is no other. I promise you. There — is — no — other!

Scene Nine

SARAH's *flat. Everyone is there surrounding and listening to* ROSA. *Only* GERDA *is apart and bandaged on a couch.* ROSA *finishes relating the story. From here, this scene and all its characters must be full of energy, for these are people who eat and bustle while they talk.*

ROSA. And then I went on to talk quickly about jobs and when I left them I was so nervous and shaking that I had to rush to the lavatory to be sick. So feeble. So bloody feeble.

BOOMY. And you'll lose the job?

ROSA. With luck, yes. You're not supposed to talk like that to the pupils.

(*Silence.*)

SARAH. Good! *You* were sick? Gerda here got a good bashing? Let's eat!

RUDI. And the 'Succah'? We made a 'Succah'. I don't know why we made it—I mean who's orthodox? I'm not orthodox, I'm just Jewish. But we made it! So now what do we do with it?

(RUDI's *question brings everything to a halt.*)

TERESSA. We've got no cuples, we've got no prayer books.

ROSA. It was only meant to be a gesture.

SARAH. To please Gerda.

TERESSA. And *is* Gerda pleased?

GERDA (*Too late for anything to please her*). And is Gerda pleased!

TERESSA. It's sacrilegious. I mean, we don't even remember.

RUDI. Doesn't anyone remember?

SARAH. Who can remember? We were children.

EMANUEL (*reading from the little book*). 'The "Succah" gave ample opportunity for hospitality, and in the words of the Zohar (*directing this at* BOOMY): "It is necessary for man to rejoice within the 'Succah' and show a cheerful countenance to guests." '

BOOMY. So? What you waiting for? Go inside. We'll pass you in some food, you start eating and then you show a cheerful countenance to the guests!

EMANUEL (*continuing reading*). 'It is forbidden to harbour thoughts of gloom and, how much more so, feelings of anger within the portals of the "Succah" — the symbol of joy.'

BOOMY. Joy! Joy! You know what book belongs to 'Succous'? Ecclesiastes! So! Go read Ecclesiastes and be joyful!

JACK. Perhaps I should go.

SARAH. Not you. You're the guest.

BOOMY. To whom must be shown the cheerful countenance.

EMANUEL. And a fat lot of cheer he or anyone'll get from you! Sarah, is the water hot for a bath later?

SARAH. What kind of a question's that? The water's always hot.

ROSA (*who's taken the little book from* EMANUEL). A procession. It says you must make a procession.

SARAH. Still not eat?

ROSA. You wanted to celebrate 'Succoth'? Then follow the instructions.

BOOMY (*sitting*). I'm not going to be party to such mockery, to such irreverence, to such childishness.

EMANUEL (*sitting*). Nor me!

BOOMY (*standing*). Maybe I'll change my mind.

EMANUEL (*standing*). See how easy it is to get him to do things?

ROSA (*reading*). 'Josephus in his work *The Antiquities of the Jews* stated that during the offering of the sacrifices in the Temple "everyone of the worshippers carried in his hands a branch of myrtle and willows joined to a bough of the palm tree, with the addition of the citron".' Here, Mother, you can hold the lemon.

SARAH. I'm beginning to feel embarrassed.

TERESSA. I must tell you, I think we should only do this in a synagogue, not in a home.

ROSA. 'The Talmudic regulations which give detailed instructions as to how the plants should be held indicate that the custom of "Waving" the plants and of bearing them whilst in procession during the service was widely in use before Mishnaic times.'

(ROSA *meanwhile has been giving everyone a branch of some sort to hold in their hand.*)

MILLIE. We going somewhere?

RUDI. So! We walk and wave the branches. (*He begins to move and waves his branch. Everyone slowly, awkwardly, self-consciously, follows him. They move in a circle.*)

RUDI. Then what?

TERESSA. But we've got no service.

RUDI. Who knows the service?

TERESSA. In a synagogue they'd know the service.

MILLIE. Where we going?

BOOMY. You don't even know what it all stands for do you?

EMANUEL. Tell us, O wise one.

BOOMY. It's man. Every different plant stands for a different part of the body. The palm is the spine, the myrtle is the eyes, the willow is the lips.

JACK. Beautiful.

ROSA. And the lemon?

BOOMY. I don't know.

GERDA. The lemon is the heart. Bitter.

EMANUEL. Nonsense! It represents the unity of differences.

BOOMY. The unity of differences!

EMANUEL. The unity of different abilities and different races — that's what it means. Judaism was a universal religion.

BOOMY. That's what those German Jews said. Trying to make themselves acceptable to everyone.

(*Everyone is brought to an abrupt halt.*)

ROSA (*reading*). 'Rabbenu Bahya ben Asher, the medieval moralist, utilizes the Succah to emphasize the profound lesson that symbols which have their roots in the ancient past must not be regarded as obsolete tradition but as observances which require renewal of interest and enthusiasm and even of language and terminology, to engage the minds of new generations.' That's me! *I'm* supposed to tell you what to do?

(*Pause.*)

GERDA. Sing. Perhaps you should sing?

EMANUEL. Now that's a good idea.

BOOMY (*throwing down his branch*). Madness!

SARAH. Let's eat.

(*Everyone takes a place at the table.*)

ROSA (*to* GERDA). We tried.

GERDA. I'm grateful.

BOOMY. 'Then I beheld all the work of God, that a man cannot find out the work that is done under the sun; because though a man labour to seek it out, yet he shall not find it; yea farther, though a *wise* man think to know it, yet shall *he* not be able to find it.' Ecclesiastes.

EMANUEL (*preparing to light the candles*). 'For wisdom is a defence, even as money is a defence; but the excellency of knowledge is, that wisdom giveth life of them that have it.' (*Pause.*) Ecclesiastes!

(EMANUEL *lights the candles.*)

BOOMY. There's no cover on his head, no prayer on his lips and he's lighting candles.

EMANUEL. My head is covered with grey hairs and there are more prayers on earth than was ever dreamt of in Heaven.

ROSA. Enough, Uncle Manny. Let's eat.

EMANUEL. I was mad! All my life I've been depressed. Depressed! What was I depressed for? Sarah, is the water hot for a bath later?

SARAH. I've told you! It's hot, it's hot. What's the matter with him?

EMANUEL. And so one morning I woke up and I said, 'Manny,' I said, 'you're not young any more!' And I went out and bought myself a tape-recorder and started singing. And you know what? I got a good voice. Pass the salt someone, please.

BOOMY. Brother mine, answer me a question. Do I exist?

EMANUEL. Do you what?

BOOMY. Exist.

EMANUEL. I sometimes wonder.

BOOMY. Prove it.

EMANUEL. Prove what?

BOOMY. That I exist.

EMANUEL. You doubt it?

BOOMY. I doubt it.

EMANUEL. So! You exist.

BOOMY. That's not evidence, that's faith.

EMANUEL. You idiot, you. The fact that you doubt is proof that you exist because you exist to doubt it.

BOOMY (*arrested*). Mmm. I'll come back on it.

EMANUEL (*reaching for a tape-recorder*). Who would like to hear me sing?

SARAH. Not now.

GERDA. Look at him, it's not fair, such energy.

EMANUEL. 'What've you been depressed about?' I said.

GERDA. I grow old and he grows young.

EMANUEL. 'What! You've committed crimes? You've done harm? Betrayed people? Alright!' I said, 'so the world's got troubles, but someone's got to remember how to be happy. You mustn't lose the habit of joy,' I said. 'Someone's got to carry it around.'

66

GERDA. So they chose my Manny.

EMANUEL. People need it!

GERDA. People! People! Don't talk to me about people.

EMANUEL. Seventy years a madman.

GERDA. There's a silliness, a—a—nastiness to people which—
Ach! Explain to them, tell them things—for what? What
do they understand? A little bit of niceness? Kindness?
Nothing! Nothing they feel and nothing they know.
Hot angers they've got, about grubby little things.
So leave me alone about people, all my life I've had
people.

(EMANUEL *goes to her, partly to pacify her, partly to bring
some food.*)

EMANUEL. Eat! Eat and be happy!

GERDA. Look at him. I grow old and he grows young.

EMANUEL. Shuh! Shuh!

TERESSA. That's what makes you grow old, darling. Eating!
We eat too much *and* the wrong things. The body works
overtime. Eat the wrong things—your body works the
wrong way. Look at Shaw, a vegetarian, lived to nearly
a hundred.

EMANUEL. And did you read about those farmers in Georgia?
Honey and yoghurt—lived till a hundred and forty.

JACK. I think it's sex.

TERESSA. Did he say 'sex'?

JACK. Sex makes you grow old. It's been proved. Look at
nuns and monks. Beautiful.

BOOMY. And *I* think it's just living. The longer you live, the
older you get!

MILLIE. Me, I've got three grandchildren, a boy, a girl, a boy;
and listen what happened. It was after a bath and the girl
put her hand between her legs and said—this is children
for you—she said, 'I'm only nine and I've already got
hairs.' And so the youngest, of course, had to say something, and so he looked and found four or five; but the

eldest, the eldest says, 'Well, what about me, I'm only ten and I've got a forest!'

(*General laughter.*)

TERESSA. My grand-daughter calls them 'public hairs'.

ROSA (*to* SARAH). *Your* grand-daughter asks me to lend her the nail varnish because she wants to paint her 'testicles'!

(*Great laughter.*)

TERESSA. Ah! Laughter, laughter, laughter! You know, on the Continent they think the Englishman is a very humourless animal.

JACK. You can't beat an English joke!

TERESSA. I'm not talking about jokes. Jokes are jokes, little stories, nothing important; but humour, real humour, to look at a situation and find humour *in* it — *that* the Englishman can't do.

BOOMY. Nonsense! You've never heard of English satire?

TERESSA. Oh, he can mock. Very good at mocking. And being rude.

BOOMY. Look at more television. That's where you'll see what makes the Englishman laugh.

TERESSA. Precisely! Rudeness! Someone insults someone else — they laugh! Someone punches someone else — they laugh! A husband calls his wife a nit — big, big laughter! Very subtle! And now it's sexual jokes. The Englishman has to prove he's sexy, so there's innuendos about things that stand up and fall down. Stand up, fall down, put in, take out. All very subtle.

RUDI. I'm missing somebody. Rosa. Your husband the soil expert. (*Pause.*) Have I said something wrong?

ROSA. You've said nothing wrong, but my husband the soil expert is trying to cross an oak with a rose to strengthen the one and colour the other and he's not having much luck. All he can produce is mud.

RUDI. And where is Martin? (*Pause.*) Have I said something else wrong?

BOOMY. Your cousin! Huh! Have you got a cousin.

RUDI. I've said something wrong.

ROSA. Your cousin is on his way to prison.

RUDI. Nobody tells me anything.

ROSA. He'll spend six months in prison because our uncle there thinks it'll make him a *mensch*.

RUDI. Who says prison makes a *mensch*?

BOOMY. He'll learn: you can't apply to Britain what you can in other countries.

RUDI. That's a funny idea that is to think prison makes a *mensch*.

BOOMY. A thousand years this country hasn't been occupied. A thousand years to grow, unmolested — it means something. You can't change it overnight.

RUDI. You let your son go to prison to be made a man?

BOOMY. He wants to change Britain? Good! Find other ways. He'll spend six months in jail and come out a *mensch*.

RUDI. Funny ideas people have.

BOOMY. Rudi, you're a fool.

RUDI. Don't call me a fool. Nobody calls me a fool.

SARAH. Stop it, enough now.

BOOMY. I've got a family of fools.

RUDI. Anybody calls me a fool and they know what's coming, you know what I mean?

BOOMY (*mocking*). 'You know what I mean?'

RUDI. You had a clever son, educated, I wish I was educated like him, what did you send him to prison for?

BOOMY. What did *I* send him to prison for!

RUDI. One day he comes to me and he says, 'Rudi,' he says, 'there's a fortune to be made out of simple ideas.' 'What's simple about anything?' I tell him. 'Listen,' he says. 'Look around you. What doesn't function properly?' Funny question. 'The lights work,' I say. 'The trains run on time, or nearly always,' I say. 'The planes stay up in the air, the clock goes,' you know what I mean?

BOOMY (*mocking echo*). 'You know what I mean?'

RUDI. 'No, no!' he says. 'Simple things! Simple things!'
'Alright!' I say, '*you* tell me.' 'A nut-cracker,' he says.
'You ever seen a nut-cracker that cracks nuts properly?'
You ever hear? 'In this day of rockets to the moon,' he
says, 'they haven't got a tool to crack nuts!' Of course, I
knew what he was talking about because I've studied
electronics, studied it, you see. So then he says, 'I'm going
to go to a nut-cracking factory and find out how they do
it. But', he says, 'they won't part with their secrets so I've
got to pretend I'm a school-teacher and take a party of
kids on a trip.' So what does he do? He rounds up half a
dozen kids, gives them five shillings each to play truant
and takes them to a nut-cracking factory.

(*Silence. Everyone waits.*)

BOOMY. So?

RUDI. So what?

BOOMY. So what happened?

RUDI. How should I know what happened? *You* sent him to
prison. I haven't seen him again. I never see this family
except once in a blue moon when I go to *them*. I'd die and
no one would visit me.

(EMANUEL *and* GERDA *have been whispering together in
subdued tones. Suddenly their conversation erupts.*)

EMANUEL. And I'm telling you I *will* be cremated.

GERDA. Never! You can stand on your head but you'll lie
by *me* when you're dead.

EMANUEL. And if *you* die first I'll make my own arrangements.

GERDA. And if *you* die first?

EMANUEL. The arrangements are made.

GERDA. I'll change them. We slept together alive? We'll
sleep together dead.

EMANUEL. Countermand my orders and you'll be dishonour-
ing the dead.

GERDA. Why didn't you tell me?

EMANUEL. A dozen times I've told you.

GERDA. Never! You've never said a word till now.

EMANUEL. You don't listen.

GERDA. We've paid for the plots.

EMANUEL. *You've* paid for the plots.

GERDA. Cremated! Dust!

EMANUEL. Ashes.

GERDA. Ashes! In the wind. Nothing left.

EMANUEL. You think I'll stay whole in the earth?

GERDA. I won't let it happen. I want you by me. You'll see.

EMANUEL. *You'll* see.

GERDA. All these years paying for nothing.

EMANUEL. I'm going to have a bath. A lovely supper but you'll excuse me, please.

(*Storms off.*)

SARAH (*calling after him*). *Now* you're quarrelling with her?

GERDA. Leave him. He needs a bath. May it be too hot for him, then he'll know about cremation.

TERESSA. As if there isn't enough violence in the world!

BOOMY. Violence! Violence! Everyone's talking about violence—a big mystery! What causes it! Whisper, whisper, whisper, psssssss! Why don't they ask me? Ask me, I'll tell them.

(*Silence.*)

ROSA (*finally*). We're asking you, Uncle Boomy.

BOOMY. What! They've never heard of cultural intimidation?

ROSA. Whew!

BOOMY. I'm not of course referring to your so-called 'magnificent primitive working man'—we all know nothing can intimidate him. I'm referring to the men of *real* inferiority, men who suspect their own stupidity. That's where violence comes from. The anger of self-knowledge. Self-knowledge that he's a pig and then—everything intimidates him: a tone of voice, a way of dressing, a

71

passion for literature, a passion for music, for anything! He hates it! One little speck of colour on a man's personality unleashes such venom, *such* venom. Money he has, security, a good job, a house, a car—everything. Not riches, I'm not talking about riches, but like us—enough. And still, and yet, his whole body, every corpuscle in his thick blood is on fire and alive to the slightest deviation *from what he is*. Can't bear it! Grrrr! Hit it! Smash it! He'll show who's superior and who's not. Wham! And there it is, all around him, the intimidation—bookshops, television, flamboyant actresses, Cabinet ministers who went to university, protesting students with long hair, trade-union leaders with big cars, black leaders with clenched fists, pop singers, Hippies, Yippies, Queers, Yids! 'Know thyself!' everyone says. 'Unto thine own self be true!' What's that for advice? We *know* ourselves. Only too bloody true we know ourselves. That's the trouble. We know ourselves too well. Grrrr! Can't bear it! And there they are, the intimidated, squirming in their factories and shops, missing it all. The adverts tell them! Missing it and hating it and hating themselves for missing it. Trapped! All over the place, in little black holes, trapped! Grrrr! Who can I smash? Who's fault is it? Someone's got to suffer as well as me. Wham! Nigger, Jew, Artist, Student. Lynch 'em! Send 'em back! Bring back the gallows, the whip, anything. I—hate—them! I—hate—me! Hate! Grrrrr! (*Pause.*) Violence? They want to know about violence? Me! Ask me.

(*Silence.*)

SARAH. Boomy, you're a very depressing man.

(*Silence.*)

JACK. Dogs! Have yous ever thought about dogs?

TERESSA. Dogs? Did he say dogs?

JACK. Do you know a dog has a smell wot's a hundred times more sensitive than ours? Fact! So, wot's old Jack been thinking to hisself? Can you not, he thinks, can you not give a dog music through smells?

TERESSA. Music? Did he say music?

JACK. Take an organ. Wot does an organ do? A piano you knocks, but an organ you puffs. I knows, yer see, 'cos I used to work where they made 'em. You puffs out air and yer puts a tube in the way. And if yer puts a big tube in the way it makes one kind of sound and if yer puts a small tube in the way it makes another kind of sound. Now, suppose yer puffs through your tube and yer puts a special *smell* in the way?

TERESSA. Is he serious?

JACK. A different smell, like a different note. And if the tube is big yer puff a big smell and if the tube is small yer puff a small smell. And music makes yer *feel* things, same as smells, so—smells can be puffed out to make a dog feel things.

TERESSA. He *is* serious.

JACK. Would not that, I ask you, breed a special kind of dog? (*Silence.*)

MILLIE. He's a very funny man.

TERESSA. Yes, well, everybody's got a funny something with them. You need it! To survive! I tell you—I escaped from the Germans in the war, with my family. We went to live for a little while in Denmark. Did I say 'live'? Hide! Who could live in Europe during the war? Anyway, with me was a mad woman and she was also Jewish; but beautiful? Like you've never seen. And—*she* was lucky. A famous Danish poet—he's dead now but I won't mention names— an old man, about sixty-five, agreed to marry her to save her from the Gestapo. Only once they married she began to claim her conjugal rights! What do you think! An old man of sixty-five and she began to make demands like that on him. It's not a joke. 'I insist,' she used to say, 'I insist that he honours me with the traditional performance in bed.' And she used to whip him with her breasts, beat him, a poet! This little woman! On the run from the gas chambers! Making love! I ask you!

ROSA (*rising*). A toast! Ladies and gentlemen, a toast! In the eighteenth century in France there was a famous woman called Madame d'Epinay. And she was the centre of great learning and great men. Among the many ways she helped them was to keep up a correspondence with some of them. But one by one they died, those keen minds of Europe, and she became sadder and sadder. But with one, a lively Abbé in Italy called Abbé Galiani, she maintained the longest and probably the last of her letter-writings. And as those great men about her died, she reported it to the Abbé and she wrote: 'I'm made of iron. Everything hurts me, nothing kills me.' To my mother.

(*Everyone rises.*)

ALL. To Sarah!

SARAH. Me? Me?

(JACK *has been fiddling with the tape-recorder and suddenly we hear* 'MANNY' *singing.*)

JACK. It works!

ROSA. Leave it playing.

(ROSA *takes a table-napkin and offers an end to her mother. The others join in humming and clapping while she and* SARAH, *shyly, begin a delicate Hasidic dance.*
Suddenly EMANUEL *bursts in covered by a towel. He rushes to switch off the tape-recorder.*)

EMANUEL. I got it! I got it! The answer! Listen everybody, I've been thinking and I've been thinking and at last it's come to me. In the bath.

GERDA. He'll catch cold the lunatic.

EMANUEL. Evil! It doesn't exist. It can't.

BOOMY. He's a tryer. I'll say that for him.

EMANUEL. Listen! Evil is when you want to be cruel—right? And cruelty—now listen carefully—(*slowly*) cruelty is

74

when one man is trying to create a situation in which *he* is not suffering pain.

(*Silence.*)

GERDA. I didn't hear.

EMANUEL. Cruelty is when one man is trying to create a situation in which *he* is not suffering pain.

BOOMY. What new nonsense is this?

(*General commotion, everyone asking each other what he means.*

JACK *decides at this moment to leave, as though it's all too much for him.*)

ROSA. Uncle Manny, it's brilliant.

BOOMY. It's nonsense!

GERDA. Go back to your bath, you'll catch cold.

EMANUEL. You don't understand, you're not listening. Don't you realize the significance of what I'm saying?

JACK (*on his way out, ringing*). Jack's a-dying, the young folk is living, Jack's a-going, the young folk is coming.

SARAH. Jack! Jack! Supper isn't over yet. (*But he's gone.*) It's like a madhouse here.

EMANUEL. Think about it, for Christ's sake, think about it.

BOOMY. What? What? Think about what? 'Vanity of vanities, all is vanity.'

ROSA. What's vanity got to do with Uncle Manny's definition of cruelty?

BOOMY. 'A fool's voice is known by a multitude of words.'

ROSA. But his definition was brief, very succinct, don't be so ungenerous.

BOOMY. 'Better is a handful with quietness than both the hands full with travail and vexation of spirit.'

EMANUEL. I produce an original thought and he quotes me Ecclesiastes.

BOOMY. 'The thing that hath been it is that which shall be,
And that which is done is that which shall be done,
And there is no new thing under the sun.'

TERESSA. It's very beautiful.

EMANUEL. I know it's beautiful but I can't bear people who quote it all the time. You have to earn the right to find the world a vain place. But he *enjoys* quoting it, he *loves* it, relishes it. Listen to him roll all that juicy gloom on his lips. 'All things toil in weariness' — aaaah! All things, that is, except *him*. You don't catch him reciting wearily — no! There's an energetic ecstasy in *his* voice. He *loves* it. Pronouncements of doom. Revelations of futility. Declarations of life's purposelessness. Except for *him*. *He's* got a purpose. A lovely purpose. The easiest of all purposes — to inform that no purpose exists! Catastrophemonger!

GERDA. He'll have a heart attack, I promise you.

EMANUEL. *He's* made no impression on the world? So! It's a flat and dreary world. *He's* failed to live a life he can respect? So! It's a vain life. *He's* approaching death? Therefore it must all have been for nothing.

GERDA. Go back to your bath, you'll catch cold.

EMANUEL. No one wants to die, *I* know that; it's a rotten time, old age; just when you're at peace you've got to go. But *that's* a reason to plague youth with our disappointments? We must warn them before they begin that it'll all be for nothing?

BOOMY. 'Rejoice, O young man, in thy youth;
And let thy heart cheer thee in the days of thy youth,
And walk in the ways of thine heart,
And in the sight of thine eyes ... '

EMANUEL. It's as though he doesn't listen.

BOOMY. 'But know thou that for all these things
God will bring thee into judgement ... '

EMANUEL. Let them read it later, when it's got meaning for them.

BOOMY. 'Therefore remove sorrow from thy heart,
And put away evil from thy flesh;
For childhood and youth are vanity.'

EMANUEL. CATASTROPHEMONGER! (*He begins to press* BOOMY *round the room*.) 'The chef who day-dreams his dishes, must he love those who eat them?'

BOOMY. He *never* gives up.

EMANUEL. And if some are indifferent to his tastes, must he cease to concoct them?

BOOMY. More nonsenses.

EMANUEL. Quiet. It's my turn to quote. 'The architect who designs houses, and plans cities, must he love those who dwell in them? And if the inhabitants are blind to the city's beauties, must the architect offend his own sight and create monstrosities?'

BOOMY. What's this got to do with anything?

EMANUEL (*pressing him on*). 'If a man reasons and struggles to legislate for the well-being of his neighbours, must he needs love all his neighbours? And if they are insensitive to the change he has helped bring to their lives, must he cease to reason for that change? If all action seems vain, must we cease all action?

BOOMY. Come to the point.

EMANUEL. I tell you verily — verily I tell you — he has no choice. The chef, the architect, the man of reason, do what they must because men must apply what is in them to apply. And so — '

BOOMY. And so, and so?

EMANUEL. 'And so, to cry "vanity of vanities" at foolish or evil men and then to abandon your true work is to abandon not them but yourself; it is to be guilty of an even greater vanity: for you knew what they did not.'

BOOMY. Who said all that?

EMANUEL. Guess.

BOOMY. Joke me no jokes, who said it?

EMANUEL. Me!

BOOMY. You?

(MANNY *dances off in his bath towel which he daringly*

77

throws open to defiantly reveal his backside — like a can-can dancer.)

EMANUEL. Me! Me! Meeeeee!

(*On his way out he turns on recorder of himself singing.*)
And listen to that!

(ROSA *jumps up again. Again she flicks the napkin to* SARAH *who rises and again — the dance. Slowly, slowly and sweetly — to the low humming and clapping of the others, while* BOOMY *calls after* EMANUEL — *who continues to laugh and mumble, 'Me, me, mee', creating a contrapuntal background to:*)

BOOMY. 'Because to every purpose there is a time and judgement, therefore the misery of man is great upon him. For he knoweth not that which shall be; for who can tell him when it shall be? There is no man that hath power over the spirit to retain the spirit, neither hath he power in the day of death … '

The LIGHTS *have been slowly* DIMMING *on the dancing and the shouting and the singing.*

Now —

THE CURTAIN

Quotations from Ecclesiastes

Act One

Page 16: 'It is better to hear ... the song of fools.' Chap. vii, 5.
Page 18: 'I Kahelth ... vexation of spirit.' Chap. i, 13–14
Page 32: 'That which is crooked ... increaseth sorrow.'
  Chap. i, 15 and 18

Act Two

Page 65: 'Then I beheld ... to find it.' Chap. viii, 17 'For
  wisdom ... that hath it.' Chap. vii, 12
Page 75: 'A fool's voice ... words.' Chap. v, 3
  'Better is a handful ... vexation of spirit.' Chap. iv, 6
  'The thing ... under the sun.' Chap. i, 9
Page 76: 'Rejoice ... sight of thine eyes. But know thou ...
  into judgement. Therefore remove sorrow ... youth are
  vanity.' Chap. xi, 9–10
Page 78: 'Because to every purpose ... day of death.' Chap.
  viii, 6–8